Simple Gifts

Other books by this author: *Scraps of Wisdom From Grasshopper Junction*

To order, call 1-800-765-6955.
Visit us at www.reviewandherald.com for information on other Review and Herald® products.

Simple Gifts

Savoring Life's Essentials

Leslie Kay

REVIEW AND HERALD® PUBLISHING ASSOCIATION
HAGERSTOWN, MD 21740

This book was
Edited by Richard W. Coffen
Copyedited by Jocelyn Fay and James Cavil
Designed by Tina M. Ivany
Cover art by photographer Andy Caulfield/The Image Bank/
    Getty Images
Electronic makeup by Shirley M. Bolivar
Typeset: Bookman Light 10/14

PRINTED IN U.S.A.

07 06 05 04 03   5 4 3 2 1

R&H Cataloging Service
Kay, Leslie Eileen, 1957-
    Simple gifts.

    1. Religious life.   2. Spiritual life.
I. Title.

248

ISBN 0-8280-1696-8

Dedication

To Dad,
a lover and teller of stories
who never lets the facts
get in the way of a good one,

And to Mom,
whose generosity and encouragement
have helped make our
good life even better.

Acknowledgments

"An Invitation to Sweep Us Off Our Feet" read the ad. Intrigued, I studied the details—"Next year's *Review* has a couple openings for monthly columns," it declared, "and you're invited to vie for a spot."

Hey, I thought, as I laid down the September 1996 issue of the *Adventist Review, I guess that includes me.* And I sent a proposal for a gospel-centered column along with three stories featuring Thelma, our intractable guinea hen; Jake, our voracious pound puppy; and our talkative toddler, Jenny. *If nothing else, maybe the editors will get a good laugh out of them,* I thought.

They did more than laugh. Amazingly, then assistant editor Andy Nash, editor William Johnsson, and the editorial staff embraced the idea. And so was born the column On the Home Front, from which most of the material in this book has been derived.

My heartfelt thanks to the entire *Adventist Review* staff for taking a chance on an old hippie from Chloride, Arizona. You've entrusted me with the privilege of sharing the joys and burdens of my heart with my brothers and sisters in Christ. And I have never been the same.

Contents

Preface

"Slow Down, You Move Too Fast"

Arnold Dyer knows what it means to take life slowly. Raised on a farm outside Paw Paw, Michigan, with no electricity or running water, our friend came of age in a time when folks worked long and hard just to maintain a hand-to-mouth existence. But they did it all at a pace and in a manner that gave them time to visit, to think, and to rest.

"We worked hard," he reminisced to me recently, "but we weren't in a hurry. We knew what we had to do and how much time it'd take to do it. For instance, it took us two hours to drive a team of horses four miles to the woodlot. We had time to holler at our neighbors as we were goin' by. Us kids could get out and run alongside the wagon, lookin' for fox or mink tracks—a mink'd bring $30 those days, you know, when wages were only 75 cents a day."

I listen, entranced, as Arnold introduces me to a world that will never be mine; a world he knows will never again be his. But he's eager to share, and I'm eager to learn. And against the almost overmastering current of our frenetic, hyperstimulated culture, my husband and I have determined to slow down, turn around, and make the best of that world our own.

We've determined, by God's grace, to take time to visit and to plant, to read and to build; to take time to hang our clothes on the line; to make time to draw near to God so we can know and serve Him better.

We're convinced that the crazier the world gets, the more sane and at peace we must become. So we look forward to Christ's coming to give us hope and direction, and we look back at our heritage to give us stability and perspective. In so doing, we're discovering what we believe to be the principles of the good life that God has always meant for us to live.

We must remember who we are and who God is. "Be still, and know that I am God; I will be exalted among the nations, I will be exalted in the earth," declares our Lord (Ps. 46:10, NIV). We must ever remind ourselves that we exist, not to make a name for ourselves, but to exalt our Savior and Creator and to give glory to Him. Appreciating this puts all human striving in perspective.

" 'Tis a gift to be simple, 'tis a gift to be free." To work hard and sleep deeply; to be warm and clothed and comfortable; to eat well of good nourishing food— what does it really take to be content? When Christ is given preeminence, the urgent and insatiable wants of the human heart are stilled. Covetousness and materialism give way to simplicity, contentment, and freedom, including freedom from enslaving debt and overwork.

"Won't you be my neighbor?" We yearn for the opportunity to share the gospel with our secular-minded neighbors. Until they're ready to receive it, we can still be the best of friends, sharing fresh eggs and garden produce, welding a broken water trailer, pulling a truck out of a sandy wash. We can exchange Christmas presents and attend each other's birthday parties. We can let them know we care about and pray for them, and leave the results in God's hands.

"Keep Manhattan, just give me that countryside."
Organic gardening, fresh eggs, a growing identification
with the rhythms and cycles of nature; we're learning
so much. And still to come: canning and dehydrating,
fruit and nut trees, a greenhouse. Nature really is God's
second, wonderfully restorative, book.

We're making progress. Even so, impatient baby
boomers that we are, we often bemoan how long it's
taking us to slow down—*40-plus years old, and we're
still not where we want to be!* When Arnold hears that,
he gently chides from his vantage point of eight produc-
tive decades, "When I was 40 years old, I realized it
took Moses 40 years to get a worldly education, and another 40 years before the Lord could use him. And I
saw that I was no different than Moses. So I realized
that, at 40, I was just getting started in life. You two got
a long way to go yet."

A long way to go—and we're going to take our time
getting there.

Saying the B Word

Bankruptcy is an unlikely place to begin a book about the good life. It's an embarrassing admission, to say the least, and not one that's calculated to earn me any credibility as a voice of Christian integrity. Yet despite the embarrassment, and because I hope that someone may be helped through my experience, I've chosen to be candid and let the credibility factor fall where it will. This story begins with bankruptcy.

Six years ago when my husband, Don, and I staked our claim, so to speak, on the old silver mine we now call home, it wasn't with the intention of going broke and declaring bankruptcy. We left our beautiful new house in Tucson and settled into a modest mobile home on the Tuckahoe[1] in a decided effort to avoid the b word. We did our best—reduced our mortgage payment by more than half, cut up our credit cards, and learned to live within our means. But it was never enough to feed the beast.

The debt we had amassed in Tucson had taken on a frightening life of its own, insatiably swallowing up nearly every drop of income Don could scrounge from his scrap metal recycling business. And soon after we moved, the Pacific Rim countries began to slip into a recession that dragged the scrap metal industry along for the ride. Sometimes prices plunged so rapidly that by the time Don had processed the scrap and sold it to the recyclers, it was worth less than he had paid for it.

We pleaded with our creditors to work with us as we struggled to stay solvent, and some did—for a time. But then an alarming thing happened. They began to raise our interest rates.

Distraught, I called one company and asked why. I was informed, "We've increased your interest rate because our credit agency has determined that you and your husband fit the profile of people about to go into bankruptcy."

Astounded, I protested, "But that's exactly what we're trying to avoid! If you raise our interest rates, you'll drive us into it!"

"I'm sorry, ma'am," the representative replied, as she probably had to a thousand other distraught callers. "That's our policy and there's nothing I can do about it."

So it went. The bills arrived like clockwork, and my husband literally ran like a rat on a treadmill to keep up with them. As the years passed, I watched him fading away under the monumental strain. As his fiftieth birthday approached he sadly confided, "Honey, I'm getting too old to work this hard. I just can't do it anymore—it's killing me."

As I looked at his haggard face and sagging shoulders, I knew it was true. And I knew we were beaten. It was time to say the b word.

We decided to wipe the slate clean and do what it took to become completely debt-free. We surrendered the mobile home with its 25-year mortgage, borrowed $7,000 from my mom, and drew up plans to build a 700-square-foot home—the largest house we could afford and the smallest we thought our family of four could cohabit without killing one another. We had just enough time to complete it before the mortgage company would arrive to cart away the mobile home. And just as it came time to begin construction, the unbelievable happened.

One sunny Sunday morning in September as I was talking long-distance with a friend, I heard a faint strangling voice calling what sounded like my name. As I turned toward the sound, I saw Don stumbling to the house, his face ashen, his right wrist cradled in his left hand. As I hung up the phone he lurched in, his face distorted with pain. We didn't need a doctor to supply a diagnosis—the bulging, grossly misshapen wrist was obviously compressed and seriously fractured.

When the self-employed, sole income earner of an uninsured family with young children becomes disabled, there is only one option. Monday morning found us being photographed and fingerprinted at the local welfare office. We would live on a monthly cash allowance of $400 plus food stamps for the next three months. But how could a right-handed man with a broken right wrist build a house? And if he couldn't, where would we live when they came to get the mobile home?

While we considered this conundrum, another crashed in on top of it. The following Sabbath we drove to the mountains to attend the worship service of our annual church campout. On the way back down the mountain, our ailing transmission locked up—for good.

Don't believe it when people say, "Well, at least things can't get any worse." They can. In one week our struggling but functioning family had been reduced to a stalled-out charity case. We had a house to build, and no way to build it; a 12-year-old car that would cost

$1,500 to repair, and no money to repair it;[2] an ancient four-speed flatbed with manual steering that neither of us could wrestle down the road. We lived 30 miles from a grocery store or gas station, and hauled our own water in a trailer that had to be pulled by the truck that neither of us could drive.

Generally it's at this juncture that human beings drop to a prone position and wail the classic "Why, God?" I think that by the time all of this had played out, I had accepted the fact that life is hard and God didn't hate us. I don't remember wailing the question "why?" so much as "how?"—how were we going to handle so much hardship at once? As it turned out, we weren't. We were going to have to pack up our pride and send it on an extended vacation while others helped us out.

We didn't even have to ask. The next Sabbath church members began stuffing $20 bills into our hands and pockets as they passed by. They slipped them to others to give to us so we wouldn't know where they had come from. A half dozen men took it upon themselves to build the forms and complete the cement work for our floor, while Don supervised with his arm in a sling. By the time his cast was removed six weeks later, our church family and friends had framed the house, built the trusses, and sheeted the roof.

As for the car, my dad lent us the money to have the transmission replaced. And we solved the truck dilemma with teamwork. Don drove and I shifted, a comical arrangement that took us to the Las Vegas Home Depot and back a number of times and still makes us laugh when we think about it.

Construction proceeded slowly for the next few

months as Don retrained his right hand to hold a hammer that weighed more than he remembered. But by the time the big trucks arrived to pack up the mobile home and drive it away, the little house was habitable. In the months following, the sale of some acreage enabled us to pay off our remaining personal debt except for the home loan—which, as of this writing, has also become history. It's a glorious feeling to be completely debt-free.

It's been an agonizing lesson—one I hope we'll never have to relearn. I've analyzed and memorized the poor planning and spending habits that created our debt monster. I've repented in tears for bringing shame to my Lord and His church. I've been humbled and subdued as I consider what our financial freedom has cost us and all those involved.

And I'm learning to pronounce, with great joy, another b word. That word is *blessed.* No matter how little I may sometimes think I have, I remind myself that I am eminently blessed. Blessed with a loving husband and two healthy children. Blessed with friends and family who care enough to help. Blessed with a Savior who casts my transgressions as "far as the east is from the west" and remembers them no more (Ps. 103:12; see Jer. 31:34).

---

[1] The Tuckahoe is a 20-acre patented silver mine in northern Arizona that we inherited from Don's father.

[2] Actually, during the course of a rather heated exchange, Don insisted that he could rebuild the transmission single-handedly—literally; at which I concluded that, while testosterone has inspired many heroic endeavors, sanity hasn't always gone along for the ride.

Counting the Cost

He sat stiffly straight by the side of the road, eyes riveted to the crest of the hill, searching for the return of the one whose tire tracks veered onto the gravel shoulder, paused, then cut a sharp U-turn. His muzzle was soft and yielding, his paws large and still unwieldy, his unkempt coat a mass of strawberry-blond curls—a half-grown, haphazard stew of Irish setter, golden retriever, and who knows what else. The girls and I passed him on our morning drive to the post office.

When we returned he had taken up his vigil in the middle of the road. Alarmed, we tried to coax him off, but he yapped and shied and parked himself a little farther down the center stripe. We prayed as a speeding truck barely missed his resolute form.

Later that day we spotted him again, now sprawled, motionless, at the base of a sign. *He's dead,* I thought angrily. *Why didn't I do something about him sooner?* I crept up to check on him. Asleep, but still very much alive, he startled and leaped away, barking furiously. Sensing that he was all bluff, I grabbed him in a bear hug and wrestled him into the wagon. We hauled him home and named him Ben.

Truth be told, I was rather proud of myself for executing such a noble rescue. In my Walter Mitty-ish inner life I thrive on ascribing to myself such grandiose titles as Defender of the Underdog and Deliverer of the

Downtrodden. But my downtrodden underdog quickly reminded me that even the noblest fantasy is a poor preparation for the rigors of real life.

Bathed, brushed, and happily gorged on puppy chow, Ben addressed his duties as family puppy with gusto. He rolled in the raised flowerbeds; he lay in the pinks; he trounced the hearts-and-flowers. He didn't just chew but actually ate anything that was not reinforced with concrete and steel. He bayed at the coyotes until I was nearly comatose with fatigue. And for an unforgettable encore he managed to get himself almost fatally run over—by me.

Came the day I'd had enough of this expensive cyclone. I told the girls in my flintiest don't-even-try-to-change-my-mind tone, "Ben has to go. I'll try to find him a new home in the morning."

They were devastated, but I was undeterred. I called every animal placement person in Kingman, who, wouldn't you know, couldn't think of anyone in need of a nondescript red puppy with a bad case of destructivitis. They'd call me if anyone turned up.

I berated myself for my stupidity: Why did I ever bring this mongrel home? What was I thinking of? Why do I feel compelled to save every stray dog in Mohave County? I prayed that a home would be found, but the call never came. Unwilling to take Ben to the pound, I reluctantly allowed him to stay. But I refused to like him.

Into my dark mutterings a new voice slowly crept, a voice that matter-of-factly convicted, *This is your pattern, you know. Thoughtlessly plunging into lives and affections; playing savior on a whim—then opting out when things get tough. When will you learn that love requires sacrifice? When will you learn to count the cost?*

This was more self-realization than I'd bargained for, but the facts spoke clearly. A marriage that had suffered from my impulsiveness; children who had been disappointed by my inconstancy; a Christian experience littered with unconsummated fair-weather resolutions.

Somehow I'd thought I could just sail through it all on dumb luck and enthusiasm and escape the inevitable cost—escape the sleepless nights and anxious prayers, the needs and dreams deferred; escape the plain hard work of it all. But the truth confronts like a sheer, impassable rock: Wherever there is love, there is sacrifice; where there is great love, there is a crucifixion.

Though it cost all, surely the reward is more than worth it—a marriage that stands the test of time; children who "rise up and call [us] blessed"; a Savior who "shall see the fruit of the travail of his soul and be satisfied" (Prov. 31:28, RSV; Isa. 53:11, RSV). And a pesky red dog that will never again know the pain of abandonment.

Three

Second Chance at Love

Twelve-year-old Anne Shirley was no stranger to rejection. Orphaned at the age of 2, shuffled from institution to abusive home and back again, she learned to find solace and identity in a highly developed fantasy life. Even so, when she arrived at stately Green Gables, an unexpected banquet of grace and civility to her starved sensibilities, Anne was willing to hope again—that someone would want her, would love and value her for who she was, not how much work she could do.

Then came the unbelievable news. She was not the boy her new family had "ordered" from the orphanage, and she was not wanted. Numb with grief, Anne struggled to wrap her emotions around this latest rejection. "You don't want me?" she asked plaintively. "You don't want me because I'm not a boy? I might have known this was all too beautiful to be true."

As our family breathed a collective sigh of sorrow for the tragic heroine of *Anne of Green Gables*, I was surprised by the intensity with which I identified with this desperate young orphan. Surprised, because it had been more than 20 years since that same sense of rejection had pervaded my own childhood and adolescence. Yet the sense and its attendant images are conjured again so readily.

Watching Anne, I saw myself—lonely and confused, shivering in the parking lot of a deserted Greyhound bus station. Summoning the scant emotional resources of my 16 years, I swallowed back tears as my father and I murmured goodbyes. I had been so happy to be with him for the past eight months; so grateful for a respite from the continual conflict that plagued my relationship with my mother. Now my stepmother, jealous of the closeness my father and I shared, had made it clear that I was no longer welcome in her home. So I kissed my dad goodbye and boarded the 2:00 a.m. bus back to Los Angeles, convinced that I was not really wanted anywhere on this earth.

Of all the stings and insults that pierce us in this sinful world, rejection is surely the most devastating. It's harder to bear than sickness and pain, harder than poverty and hardship. All manner of sorrow and tragedy can be borne and even surmounted if we can face them with the certainty that we are wanted and loved.

As I consider what I have devoted so much of my energy to attain—the approbation that never satisfies, the never-ending parade of things, the intimacy that mysteriously eludes—I realize that my life has been one massive treasure hunt for love. And I've wondered if it must ever be so—must the love-deprived forever devote ourselves to compensating for our lack?

I believe the answer is found in a growing understanding of what Christ accomplished on His cross: "But where sin abounded, grace abounded much more, so that as sin reigned in death, even so grace might reign through righteousness to eternal life through Jesus Christ our Lord" (Rom. 5:20, 21, NKJV).

Eternal death, and all that prefigures it in this life—lovelessness, alienation, rejection—have been superseded by the heroic achievement of the cross. Where sin reigned and ravaged at will, God's unmerited, unconditional love has "abounded *much more,*" reigning as a conquering king before whom no enemy can stand.

The practical implications of this principle are almost unbelievable. Though my feelings may deny it, faith informs me that, in fact, the power of God's love has broken the stranglehold of rejection. Where rejection "abounded" in fear and insecurity, God's grace abounds "much more," giving me power to say, "Whatever I've received at the hands of human beings, in Christ I am infinitely loved and cherished. In Christ I'm free to hope again, to trust again. In Christ I have a second chance at love."

I also have a second chance at happiness with a man who is devoted to me despite my considerable flaws. A second chance at childhood as I love my children through their own. And I know I'm the recipient of pure "abounding" grace when my daughter surprises me with the assurance "You know what, Mom? I'd rather be with you than with kids my age," and explains this astounding fact with a simple "'cause you're my mom."

Second chances are the most appreciated of all.

Four

A Short Leash

Many summers ago I worked as a prep cook at the Grand Canyon. One warm, lazy afternoon off, I wandered through the village and was greeted by a strange sight. I saw a young couple huddled together, eyes riveted on a park brochure held in the man's right hand, absorbed in a discussion of the next point of interest. The man's left arm was flung out to his side, muscles tensed, hand grasping the end of a taut, vibrating leash. The leash was snapped to a halter that restrained, not an overzealous dog, but a screaming toddler who clawed wildly at the air and struggled, with every ounce of his fierce little being, to break free and hurtle headfirst through the crowd to *his* next point of interest.

At the time, I sympathized with the boy. *Imagine!* I huffed to myself. *Walking your child on a leash as though he were a dog!* I've since been grocery shopping with a slippery toddler or two, and my sympathies have shifted somewhat. But I still feel for the boy—because I also know what it's like to chafe at the end of a frustratingly short leash.

My short leash is an invisible physical limitation called asthma. As far back as I can remember, asthma and its attendant allergies have been as integral a part of my identity as my blue eyes and blond hair. I was the girl at the slumber party who went home wheezing in the morning because of the cat who'd just had kittens in the closet. The pale skinny kid in PE who couldn't run anything more strenuous than the 50-yard dash. The wannabe backpacker who fantasized about, but never actually *went,* camping because of all that insidious mold-infested, pollen-producing green stuff.

When I became a Seventh-day Adventist I felt sure the Lord would cut me loose from my short leash. I ate, slept, and prayed the eight natural remedies.* I vowed that when I was healed I would sail to the farthest corners of this darkened earth to share the wonderful news of my Savior. And to demonstrate my faith, I tossed my inhaler into the trash.

The *Reader's Digest* version (as my husband would call it) of this long melodramatic tale is this: No longer a sickly, skinny, asthmatic kid, I'm now a skinny, asthmatic, somewhat hardier version of my younger self. And I never got to carry the gospel to the farthest corners of this inhospitable allergenic earth.

What can be concluded from this daily, lifelong confrontation with weakness and limitation? Just this: While God desires me to have the best health I can possibly have in this body, He doesn't need to make me well to make me useful. He doesn't need to disregard His own divinely ordained laws of heredity to make me a partaker of His divine nature and an effective ambassador of His grace.

The marvel of Christianity is its utter lack of dependence upon favorable circumstances; its capacity to thrive in the most forbidding environment, hampered by weakness and limitation—transforming the believer and the world not from the outside in but from the inside out. The glory of Christianity is the omnipotent God subjecting Himself to the limitations imposed by His own laws of heredity, eternally identifying Himself with the frailty and affliction of the children of Adam, surrendering Himself to the outworking of our deep, inward enmity—and coming off more than conqueror.

It's an infuriating mystery to the carnal mind that "God chose the foolish things of the world to shame the wise; God chose the weak things of the world to shame the strong. He chose the lowly things of this world and the despised things . . . so that no one may boast before him" (1 Cor. 1:27, 28, NIV).

I might well wish it were otherwise. Wheezing and sneezing, itching and scratching just don't *feel* very noble and victorious. But my day of deliverance is coming. Until then I can know that my short leash keeps me near the one who grips it with divine-human empathy. And I can rejoice that "when I am weak, then I am strong," because *His* strength is made perfect in my weakness (2 Cor. 12:10, NIV).

---

* "Pure air, sunlight, abstemiousness, rest, exercise, proper diet, the use of water, trust in divine power" (*The Ministry of Healing*, p. 127).

Five

What Barbie Wouldn't Do

I should have known better; these things have a way of getting out of hand. But a torrential thunderstorm that had kept us up chasing leaks half the night had left me with a bad case of fatigue-induced sillies. At lunch I felt compelled to speak in a ridiculous falsetto that had my daughters giggling into their soup. Then from some slaphappy rogue brain cell came this assertion: "If Barbie could talk, this is what she'd sound like, you know."

My children looked at me wide-eyed. "Really, Mom?"

Somberly, I replied, "Oh, yes; I'm sure of it."

As I gazed into their rapt, unusually attentive faces, my mother's brain detected a prime Manners Moment. Seizing the opportunity, I continued in my most author-itative, best Barbie-esque manner, "Barbie would al-ways speak very politely, of course, and she would *never* slurp her soup or chew with her mouth open. Barbie is the Queen of Manners."

Sensing there was now a moral to the story, the girls balked. Exchanging sly, conspiratorial smirks, their hearts instantly beat as one in a single anarchical resolve—*Let's see how far we can take this!*

Five-year-old Jenny started the fun. Sticking out her tongue, on which perched an unsavory beige mass, she lisped, "You mean Barbie wouldn't do *this?*"

"No, Jenny," I assured. "Barbie would *not* stick out her tongue with food on it."

Emitting a strangling sound that resembled an ailing garbage disposal, Becky asked coyly, "And Barbie wouldn't do *this?*"

"No, Becky," I groaned. "Barbie would *definitely* not gargle her grape juice at the . . ."

Before I could finish, Jenny broke in with "And Barbie would never throw her soup all over the floor?"

"Jenny!" I blurted urgently. "Don't even *think* about throwing your soup on the floor!"

She didn't, thankfully. Even so, as I watched my girls gargle and slurp and cram their food into their mouths like rank Neanderthals I reflected, once again, on the breathtaking speed with which a child's attentiveness can dissolve into reckless abandon. And I was reminded, again, of the absurdity of trying to inject into living, breathing human beings the sort of plastic perfectionism that Barbie so neatly personifies.

Though my proportions have never remotely resembled Barbie's impossibly idealized ones, and my conservative wardrobe could never compare with hers for style (or skimpiness), I too have dreamed the impossible dream of perfection. Consciously and unconsciously I've poured my life into the pursuit of the perfect marriage, the production of perfect children, and the portrayal of perfect Christianity.

Only God knows why. Only He fully understands the complex grid work of genetic and environmental factors that determines who will scrutinize life through the lens of this grand obsession. I do know from experience that, absent a thorough and ongoing conversion, perfectionism with its attendant criticism and intolerance will define the Christian experience just as fully as it defined the carnal experience—in fact, much more, since it now has a moral imperative in which to wrap itself.

As good as perfectionism may look, this is what the Lord has shown me: "Christian" perfectionism is very much like a beautiful butterfly preserved in amber—apparently exquisite in every detail, and also very dead. It's the antithesis of life in the Spirit.

Real life, lived in the Spirit, is unpredictable, inconvenient, even messy. It never feels the way you thought it would. It never looks the way you think it should. When it is captured and neatly kept, its great magnanimous heart grows still and cold. But when we permit it to capture and keep *us*, it becomes the way of freedom and joy.

"Now the Lord is the Spirit, and where the Spirit of the Lord is, there is freedom." For God "has made us competent as ministers of a *new* covenant—not of the letter but of the Spirit; for the letter kills, but the Spirit gives life" (2 Cor. 3:17, 6, NIV).

Every morning I have to ask myself, What'll it be? The lonely life of the "letter" that no one, including me, can ever measure up to—or the warm, vibrant life of the Spirit, apparently flawed in the details, but effective and successful overall?

What would Barbie choose? Only Mattel knows for sure. But I have a feeling she and I won't be doing lunch together anytime soon.

The Right Stuff—Is Love

My daughter Jenny and I seldom clash, but when we do it can be an event of high drama. Recently sent to time-out for some infraction, our usually good-natured 6-year-old flung her little arms across her inflated chest, lifted her chin defiantly, and declared, "I'm not talking to you again until Dad comes home!" Clearly Jenny's acute sense of justice had been affronted, especially as that justice pertained to her all-important sense of personal honor.

As I watched my little Joan of Arc resign herself to her cruel and unjust fate, I saw what so many parents see when confronted with our children at their most unattractive—I saw myself. And it wasn't a heartwarming sight.

An accomplished martyr by the time I enrolled in kindergarten, I drove my mother crazy with my self-righteous silences, often sulking over real or imagined slights for days, even weeks. Early adolescence brought a turning point. Sent to my room to think about my sullen attitude, I clamped my skinny arms across my chest and consoled myself with this bit of defiance: "Let *her* think about it! *I'm* the one who's right!" Whereupon I was confronted with a thought that didn't originate in my mutinous mind: *You can be "right," or you can be loved—but you can't be both.*

To my sorrow, I've often rejected the warmth these

words could have brought into my life, opting instead for the chilly consolations of "being right." But marriage and motherhood have made it painfully clear that we can't encase ourselves in the armor of infallibility and expect to remain tender and vulnerable enough to give and receive love. Love for others and love of being right can never share the throne.

Seventh-day Adventists know something about all this. We know the gratifying self-esteem that comes with membership in the "right" church. We enjoy the personal and spiritual benefits that derive from right-ness—from eating right, living right, believing what's right, worshiping on the day that's right. Yet we remain, in my estimation, an incomplete and conflicted people. In our hearts we sense that being loved and loving is better than being right, but we're not quite sure how to get there from here.

We've experimented with some attractive possibili-ties. We've tried lots of slogans and programs, projects and promotions. We've tried loosening up our lifestyles and livening up our worship styles. We've tried to achieve inclusiveness by downplaying distinctiveness. But though our flight from legalism has taken us down some intriguing paths, it hasn't brought us to that longed-for promised land of love.

Yet there remains a way to love, and I believe it's the way of repentance—the way of the broken heart. It's a narrow way, because it doesn't allow for egos inflated with spiritual pride and self-sufficiency. It's a simple way, not at all dependent on money, policy, or technology. It's an apparently obscure way, because we would not sup-pose that the fragrant fruit of love springs from such an unattractive "root out of dry ground" (Isa. 53:2, NIV).

It's the way of Mary Magdalene, who loved much because her broken, appreciative heart had been forgiven much (see Luke 7:36-50). It's the way of Paul, who understood that "the greatest of these is love" because he'd first understood that he, and no one else, was "the foremost of sinners" (1 Cor. 13:13, RSV; 1 Tim. 1:15, RSV). It's the way of Daniel, who though "highly esteemed" of heaven identified himself with his erring people and interceded on their behalf: "*We* have sinned, *we* have done wrong." "*We* have rebelled against" God (Dan. 10:11; 9:15, 9, NIV).

Perhaps the last and greatest temptation of a morally informed and scripturally articulate people is the temptation to believe that the goodness we experience by association with Christ derives from ourselves. Yet this is precisely the temptation that must be overcome if we would know self-forgetful, soul-winning love. Self-righteousness must go. Spiritual self-sufficiency must go. All pride of ownership of "the truth" must go. They must give way to a corporate appreciation for the agapē of Christ so that we may lighten this dying earth with His glory and help to prepare a people for His soon return.

Seven

"Yeah, But . . ."

It's been asserted that America has become a nation of crybabies—a passel of whining, pining victims blubbering out the sordid details of our dysfunctions to any lawyer, therapist, or talk show host willing to listen. It's been argued, convincingly, that we have become a people determined to deny, at all costs, accountability for our choices, actions, and dispositions.

I'm beginning to wonder if a similar assertion could be made about the church. I wonder if, in our anxiety to become a kinder, gentler, less legalistic representation of Christ, we've unwittingly imbibed the spirit of our crybaby culture and enabled one another to become so many spiritual wimps.

How often have we cried the blues with such lyrics as:

"I'd really like to break my [smoking, eating, caffeine . . .] addiction, but I'm just so stressed right now, and besides, I have a genetic predisposition."

"I wish I wasn't so choleric and impatient, but that's my temperament and I can't help it."

"I'd like to be a more [trusting, loving, dependable . . .] person, but my father was an alcoholic and my mother was controlling and manipulative, and I just can't seem to get over it."

Those who don't know the Lord might well shield themselves from accountability with such trendy rationalizations. As far as they know, there is no one to deliver them from temptation in a godless world, and no one to run to when the heat of retribution comes searing down.

But what about the church? What have we done with our Savior? Have we eclipsed the Crucified One, the only One able to "deliver us, and purge away our sins," with so much humanistic understanding and earthbound empathy (Ps. 79:9)? Have we exchanged the empowering, objective truth of the gospel for the sweet but feeble warm fuzzies of the subjective?

Even the most earnest personal testimony of spiritual deliverance, colored as it is by the subjective, leaves room for a rueful, "Yeah, but—you don't know what it's like for *me;* you don't know what *I've* been through." And it's true. The collective mind of the Christian church can never know what it is to wrestle with *my* besetting sins, weighed down with the baggage of *my* past. The church can never know, but the Lord of the church does.

Christ not only became human *like* us; He became human *as* us. His humanity embraced not only his own individuality, but the heredity, the temperament, the life experience of everyone who has ever lived and ever will. "He took human nature, and bore the infirmities and degeneracy of the *race"* (*The Seventh-day Adventist Bible Commentary,* vol. 5, p. 1081; italics supplied). And He didn't just bear them suddenly at the cross, as one might bear a passing inconvenience. His was a developing, lifelong identification with the struggles and frailties of humanity.

By the age of 12, "the mystery of His mission was opening to the Saviour," and He began consciously to carry "the awful weight of responsibility for the salvation of men" (*The Desire of Ages*, pp. 78, 92). At 30, repenting in our behalf on the banks of the Jordan, Jesus "identified Himself with sinners. . . . As one with us, He must bear the burden of our guilt and woe. The Sinless One must *feel* the shame of sin" (*ibid.*, p. 111; italics supplied). Even then, still years away from the cross, "the sins of a guilty world were laid upon Christ" (*ibid.*, p. 112).

In His heart and in His mind, in His muscles and bones and nerves, Christ bore "the burden of our guilt and woe"; consciously, daily, continually He lived *our* struggle with deeply ingrained, even unconscious, sin— not just *for* us, but *as* us. He gazed unblinkingly into our corporate heart of darkness until He became sin itself, and was destroyed. We have nothing to bear that He has not already borne in our behalf.

Caring is good; understanding and empathy are as dew in a parched and weary land. But let's not settle for caring when we can have caring *and* cleansing. Let's not let an unbelieving "Yeah, but . . ." keep us from our Redeemer. Through the power of prayer and gospel truth, by the living witness of our own soul's surrender, let's commend each other to the One whose glory it was to become sin for us, *as* us, "that we might be made the righteousness of God in him" (2 Cor. 5:21).

Eight

Promises, Promises

C"Can I *please* get in bed with Becky for just a *little* while? We *promise* not to laugh or make any noise. Oh, *pleeeease*, Mom?"

Peering hopefully from her doorway, our daughter Jenny delivered this latest battle-of-the-bedtime stall with all the wide-eyed, winsome ingenuousness native to a 6-year-old, which is considerable. My husband and I exchanged knowing glances—a pair of giggly, sleep-shirking girls promising to cuddle in bed without becoming outrageously silly? *Uh-huh*. Like the fox promising not to eat the gingerbread man as he ferried him across the river. However convincing fox and child may sound, such promises are made to be broken—fast.

This promise was the latest in a recent slew of solemn pronouncements, all delivered with cross-my-heart conviction and designed to override my better judgment: "Can't I go outside without my jacket, Mom? I *promise* I won't get cold." (This in January.) "Can't I put my church clothes on *before* breakfast, Mom? I *promise* not to get food on them." (Has any 6-year-old *ever* accomplished this in the history of Christendom?)

Although I give my daughter high marks for good intentions, I've found that invariably Jenny's childish self-confidence far exceeds her ability to make good on her claims. My daughter hasn't yet discovered what fragile, undependable material she's made of.

Such childish self-confidence is nothing new on the home front. Many years ago, in a wilderness called Sinai, a few million well-meaning "children" sincerely promised their Father, "All that the Lord hath said we will do, and be obedient" (Ex. 24:7).

Their Father knew better. Knowing how they were formed, remembering they were but dust (see Ps. 103:14), He'd never asked them to "do" anything—except listen attentively to His voice and deeply regard the promise *He'd* given *them*.* The Lord knew that if His children would just be still long enough to consider His magnanimous deliverance from Egyptian bondage, their stubborn hearts could be softened and subdued (see Ex. 19:4). Appreciation could take the place of self-confidence, and spiritually informed commitment and cooperation could follow.

But "the people did not realize the sinfulness of their own hearts, . . . and they readily entered into covenant with God. . . . Yet only a few weeks passed before they broke their covenant . . . and bowed down to worship a graven image" (*Patriarchs and Prophets*, pp. 371, 372). How God must have longed to help His children see that "the knowledge of [their] broken promises and forfeited pledges" would only weaken their infant faith—that it would put into play a self-perpetuating dynamic of failure that would prevent them from growing up into the spiritually mature people He intended for them to become (see *Steps to Christ*, p. 47).

Of those children of Israel and of God's children today, it's been well said: "Even when [people] are willing to recognize the Lord at all, they want to make bargains with Him. They want it to be a 'mutual' affair—a transaction in which they will be considered as on a par with God. But whoever deals with God must deal with Him on His own terms, that is, on a basis of fact—that we have nothing and are nothing, and He has everything and is everything, and gives everything" (E. J. Waggoner, *The Glad Tidings,* p. 133).

I often wonder what sort of dynamic would be put into effect if enough of God's people became utterly divested of this childish penchant for making promises and bargains with God. What sort of critical mass of faith would be ignited if even a handful of God's children became deeply converted on this point—that all our wit, our wisdom, our strivings truly amount to nothing, and that Christ is and has and gives everything?

As I wonder, my persistent daughter believes she'll convince me, "Tickle me, Mom! I *promise* not to scream!" But this I've learned: 6-year-olds can't help screaming when they're tickled; foxes can't help eating gingerbread men; and even the most sincere Christian can't help breaking their well-intentioned but impotent promises of obedience. May God help us to lose confidence in our imagined righteousness so that we may appreciate *His* promises and heroic achievements in our behalf.

---

* See the Hebrew for "obey" and "keep" in Exodus 19:5. The word the KJV translates as "obey" means literally "hear"—"hear my voice." Its root is the same as for Shema—the prayer that begins: *"Hear* O Israel: the Lord our God is one Lord" (Deut. 6:4). The same root lies behind "observe" in some passages. The word translated "keep" comes from the same root and means to observe, regard, or abide by.

Nine

Savior of the World

There is a spontaneous bond of kinship between otherwise diverse people who have endured common hardships; an exclusive comradeship-in-arms that is incomprehensible to the uninitiated. Combat veterans gather to trade war stories. Middle-aged ex-jocks relive their glory days. And mothers of young children compare birth experiences—with the sort of vivid, unsparing detail that sends their blushing husbands fleeing from the room in acute embarrassment.

So it happened that my friend Camille and I (sans husbands) talked childbirth over a lunch of white corn tortillas, guacamole, and banana bread. "My first one was like medieval torture," Camille confessed, as her third little one wriggled in her arms. "After I lived through it, I had a new respect for even the wimpiest woman who's ever had a baby."

As the four oldest products of our combined adventures in childbirth giggled and scampered at our feet, Camille continued with a shudder, "It was a horrendous experience! I was totally out of control. For hours and hours I grabbed Ron by the neck and fell to the floor, crying and groveling, too scared to breathe into the contractions, fighting the pain."

"Was it different with Sirena?" I asked over a fourth slice of Camille's addictive banana bread.

"I knew I'd have to do things differently the second

time around," she answered. "With Sirena, I reminded myself that every contraction got me closer to her birth. I decided I would *love* the pain—I'd *embrace* the pain— because when it was over, I'd get a baby."

The wisdom of my friend's words impressed me deeply. The life that is quietly conceived "in the secret place" (Ps. 139:15, NIV) becomes manifest only through excruciating pain—pain that must be embraced, even loved, like a friend. Surely childbirth is a hard but holy privilege that can help us comprehend something of what our Savior has endured to bring redemption to the human race.

To the undiscerning eye, it all began unremarkably enough. A baby born in a Bethlehem stable to poor, nondescript parents, attended only by shepherds and the shrill bleating of sheep. Yet that baby carried within Him what no other human being had ever brought into this world—the corporate life of the fallen human race diffused with the very nature of God (see *Selected Messages,* book 1, pp. 250, 251).

Throughout childhood this unique life remained hidden within Him. Into adulthood, He carried it quietly, unobtrusively, as a pregnant woman carries the fragile, developing life within her. He nourished and fed it, purifying it from self, carrying it to full spiritual maturity until, in due time, that which had been conceived in Christ was ready to be made manifest to the world.

'He was not permitted to wrestle with His birth pangs in private. On His uplifted cross, in full view of every cynical, unsympathetic eye, Christ endured His monumental agony. Publicly despised and rejected, His tender spirit pierced and crushed, He was mortally stricken for our sakes, "cut off from the land of the living" (Isa. 53:8, NIV).

Yet He endured it—He embraced it—because He knew that every racking contraction that crushed out His life brought Him closer to the birth of a new and greater life—a shared life that would extend beyond Himself to suffuse the entire human race. And in sharing this life, Christ earned the right to be called "the Saviour of the world" (1 John 4:14).

"In the matchless gift of His Son, God has encircled the whole world with an atmosphere of grace as real as the air which circulates around the globe" (*Steps to Christ*, p. 68). Because of this gift, He is able to shower both saint and sinner with every material blessing necessary for life, including "the bread we eat" and "the water we drink" (*The Desire of Ages*, p. 660). Through this gift, He has delivered "justification that brings life for *all* men" (Rom. 5:18, NIV)—life filled with blessing, hope, and pardon.

And for those who, by faith, receive Christ in His fullness, there is *eternal* life—Christ's own divinely indwelt humanity. For us, there is the sometimes painful but holy privilege of having His image conceived and formed within us—that the unique life which was once hidden in Christ may become manifest to the watching world as "Christ in [us], the hope of glory" (Col. 1:27).

Ten

Eternally Relevant

Can a 23-year-old dope-smoking, rock-and-rolling New Ager from suburban southern California find Christ in the company of rural, ultraconservative, Ellen White-quoting Adventists? According to current conventional witnessing wisdom, it would seem unlikely. What would people of such diverse backgrounds and subcultures have in common? And how could the latter possibly share Christ in a relevant, meaningful way with the former?

Let me share my story.

Twenty years ago I found myself broke and hungry in the city of Omak, Washington. Day after day I hitchhiked from my campsite to the post office, hoping to find a $100 check from a friend in southern California. But I'd been high on marijuana brownies when I'd called and told her where to send it, and I'd spaced out on the zip code. So as my ill-fated check daily inched its way north, I returned to my campsite empty-handed.

On the tenth day, as I hitchhiked dejectedly back to my dwindling food supply with two cents—and no check—in my pocket, I was picked up by an unusual pair. A father and young son, dressed conservatively in long sleeves and suspenders, cheerfully welcomed me into their truck. Broke as I was, I accepted their invitation to stay at their home until my check arrived.

Ron and Katherine fed, housed, and put up with me

for two weeks, while I absorbed their unique lifestyle. I was amazed by their prayers; never had I seen anyone pray before and *after* meals—on their knees. I was amused by the quaint, organ-accompanied hymns they sang at morning and evening worship.* And I vowed I would never trade my beloved Levis for long dresses. But thanks to the Holy Spirit, I saw beyond these differences to the treasure that lay beneath the surface. I saw faces radiating peace and joy, genuine affection and appreciation between family members, and unashamed devotion to God and His truth. And this cynical, world-weary hitchhiker wanted it all, desperately.

Thank God my new friends also saw beyond our differences. They penetrated beneath my worldly, self-sufficient exterior to the earnest young seeker within. And I believe they understood a simple, profound truth—that the human heart, whatever it may cover itself with, however it may posture, never changes. It's always in need of reconciliation with its God; always craves appreciation, love, and respect; always searches for meaning and order. Because Ron and Katherine related to me on the basis of our common, essential humanity, they were able to share Christ with me in a way that was powerfully relevant to my life.

They ministered to the whole person. My friends didn't give me a glib lecture, stick a tract in my hand, and smile, "Go, I wish you well; keep warm and well fed" (James 2:16, NIV). They kindly and sacrificially attended to my basic, immediate need for food, shelter, and companionship, while addressing my deep poverty of soul.

They ministered to me through God's most effective witnessing medium, the family. When lonely, alienated people are accepted into a warm, vibrant family circle, God is brought very near. My two weeks with this friendly, consecrated family confirmed that the Spirit-filled home is "a little heaven upon earth" (*The Adventist Home*, p. 15).

They led me to the truth, then let me make my own decisions. My friends always permitted me to initiate our conversations about spiritual things; they never pressured me to pray or make commitments. They shared truth objectively and impersonally, allowing the Holy Spirit to make the application.

They bathed me in prayer. The sensitivity and insight with which my friends ministered to me, and the Presence that led me on to a complete commitment to the Lord, didn't happen in a spiritual vacuum. I know they resulted from earnest, persevering intercession.

With those who would insist that relevant, successful witnessing and fellowship are predicated on generational and cultural commonality, I beg to differ. Truth is not so weak that it must conform itself to the dictates of a fickle, self-indulgent popular culture in order to make an impression. Honest hearts will transcend their comfort zones to embrace an everlasting gospel that is shared by those who have, themselves, been transformed by it.

---

* Hymns that I have since grown to love.

Eleven

Don't Touch That Microwave!

I woke up in a cold sweat last night, my skin tingling from the haunting memory of the nightmare that woke me.

I'd dreamed I was watching a daytime talk show as the host addressed her audience: "Our program today is about women who care when the men they love have long ceased caring; who strive with all the passion of their souls in the face of their children's indifference. Women who roam the darkened hallways of their homes, alone, unappreciated, picking up socks while their loved ones sleep.

"'Women Who Clean Too Much'—that's the name of today's program."

A flurry of haggard nods and murmured assents rippled through the audience.

"Let's give a warm welcome to our special guest . . ." The host pivoted abruptly and turned her toothy sneer on—me?

Wait! This can't be happening! I'm not really here; I'm just watching!

But as I glanced down, I saw that I really was perched on one of those cheesy little studio chairs in front of a hungry-looking audience, with the solemn conviction that I was about to be served for lunch.

My host smiled ingratiatingly. "We have it from reliable sources that you're quite the little housekeeper."

"Well, I do my best," I replied modestly. "And with two small children, it's not easy. But my husband seems to be pleased with the results."

"Well, you may be able to fool your husband," she responded, with surprising venom, "but you can't fool the women of America!"

Cries of "That's right! America has a right to know!" exploded across the studio.

"So, as a woman with exemplary housekeeping habits, you won't object to our video crew paying a surprise visit to your home."

"Well, I wasn't expecting company . . ." I said a bit apprehensively.

Suddenly the studio melted away and the stage metamorphosed into my living room. I glanced around nervously. No questionable smells. The Barbies sat neatly in their pink house, clothed and in their right minds. This might work.

"Naturally, we expected the living room to be presentable. Let's move on to the kitchen. H'mmm . . . nothing obvious. We'll just do a little digging. You don't mind if we pull this little trap door open on your toaster, do you?"

"The toaster? Are you sure you want to . . ."

Fwap! Two pounds of incinerated crumbs showered to the floor, followed by three Lego brand blocks, a family of gerbils, and my car keys. So that's where they were!

"Wow, thanks. I've been looking for these forever," I gushed. But my host was not smiling. "Hah!" she cackled menacingly, directing her baleful gaze at the refrigerator.

I leaped, but too late. She wrenched open the door, exposing my most shameful secrets to the unsympathetic eyes of 13 million contemptuous housewives.

"Ah," she sneered, "just as I thought. Plasticized grape juice under the crisper, petrified pasta remnants chemically bonded to their Tupperware containers, fossilized ground beef in the deli drawer."

"Ground beef? Wait! I've been framed! I'm a vegetarian!"

"Of course, of course," she scoffed. "We'll just let our studio audience be the judge of that."

"Guilty!" they pronounced, pelting me with scouring pads.

"Just one last item of business," she murmured dangerously, lunging for the microwave.

"No! Not the microwave!" I shrieked. I hurled myself at the offending appliance, clutching it to my chest in a death grip.

That's when everything went black and I found myself in a sweaty embrace with my microwave at 2:00 this morning, shaking uncontrollably. What could have caused such a hideous dream? Was it that bedtime snack of leftover pizza?

I pulled open the door and peered inside, noting the recent explosions of mozzarella and red sauce cemented to its already colorful interior. Definitely the pizza. *Next time,* I decided, *I'll eat it cold.*

OK. I confess. The story is apocryphal. Thankfully, I never really dreamed I was a TV talk show guest. I've been spared that intrusion into my psyche. But my well-scrubbed children will confirm my charter membership in the Society of the Compulsively Clean. And my phlegmatic husband, who has never suffered from undue fastidiousness, has said it so many times he can murmur

in his sleep, "Relax, honey. It'll be there in the morning."
Which is exactly what keeps me from relaxing.

I didn't choose to be immaculately clean—or
painstakingly careful or compulsively organized or insufferably scrupulous. I didn't request to have the
weight of a world of dirt and inefficiency laid upon my
slender shoulders. But the law of genetics is a notorious nonrespecter of persons. And so I was delivered
into this world with conscientiousness encrypted on
every chromosome and particularity oozing from every
pore. I was born to be perfect.

Perfection is no picnic on a daily basis. But 40
years of its implacable demands can wear even the
most stalwart devotee to a whimpering frazzle. As I step
gingerly across the threshold of the "big 4-0," I feel the
heat of that unforgiving voice as it calls me to account.
"What have you been *doing* all these years? What have
you got to show for them?"

Not much, it seems. My personal achievement sur-
vey brings small comfort. High school graduate, the odd
college courses. No career to speak of, though I vaguely
recall being paid to interact with other adults, dressed
in clothes that didn't resemble sweat suits. But seven
years of full-time mothering have rendered that part of
my memory unreliable. As for material attainment, we
own our vehicles—a 1972 Ford pickup with advanced
rustitis and a demented 1986 Nissan Stanza; and our
property—a 20-acre defunct silver mine we didn't even
pay for.

Can these be the symbols of success? Can these be
the trophies that say to family and friends, "This
woman has arrived. She has made herself worthy of
your respect and admiration"?

"Are you kidding?" chides the voice. "Do you call these achievements? What kind of perfectionist are you?"

A tired one, I decide. A disenchanted one, badly in need of some good, encouraging news.

I remember a college Week of Prayer my husband and I attended some years ago. Our speaker, Pastor Robert Wieland, introduced his subject one evening with the provocative questions "What is the one thing in this world you can call your own? What single thing can you say you have earned by your own effort?"

Earnest replies included education . . . reputation . . . career . . . character.

Pastor Wieland countered these offerings with the assertion "All these blessings you have received by the grace of God—even, and especially, your character. The only thing on this earth you can truly say you have earned by your own effort is . . . your grave!"

Wait a minute! Forty years of good, honest perfectionism, and all I've earned is my grave? Is this supposed to encourage me? This is terrible news! What does the Lord have to say about this?

"The wages of sin is death" (Rom. 6:23, NIV). Of course, but we're not talking about sinful behavior. We're talking about the natural human drive, exaggerated in perfectionists but universally present, to derive social acceptance and a sense of self-worth from personal achievement. Achievement that may be tangible, social, intellectual, even spiritual. Isn't that all right? Isn't that normal?

"The righteous will live by faith," intones Scripture, because "everything that does not come from faith is sin" (Rom. 1:17; 14:23, NIV). So whatever proceeds from my own effort and imagined virtue, and not from faith

in the virtue and achievement of Christ, is sin and results in death?

Where does that leave me? I came into this world
innately programmed to secure the good opinion of my
peers, respect for myself, even my salvation by my best
efforts. Yet those efforts, springing from a fallen, fear-
based nature, carry within them the very seeds of failure, and even death.

Thank God, He loves me too much to let me lan-
guish in this cycle of death. On His cross He set the
captives free—and "if the Son sets you free, you will be
free indeed"; "free from the law of sin and death" (John
8:36; Rom. 8:2, NIV). Free from the tyranny of perfectionism, from the voice of the accuser, from the symbi-
otic motivations of pride and fear. Free from the
relentless compulsion to validate myself, justify myself,
redeem myself.

Free to be compelled by a new force—appreciation
for the agapē of Christ, the constant, unwavering
Source of my self-respect (see 2 Cor. 5:14, NIV). Free at
40, as at 4, to rest in the completeness of my Savior
and *His* perfect redemptive achievement.

Twelve

On the Evil and the Good

The throbbing of tom-toms and the cloying scent of marijuana hung about my head as I crammed my few belongings into my backpack. Hefting the oversized beast onto my slender shoulders, I fairly staggered down the mountain path, past free-spirited flower children and chanting Hare Krishnas. It was July 1978. I was leaving Oregon's Umpqua National Forest and the Rainbow Family's[1] annual gathering; heading to the highway to catch a ride north to the cherry orchards, where I hoped to find work.

In Roseburg I stowed the leaden pack against a darkened wall and crossed the road to a hamburger joint. While I munched, I kept a watchful eye on my backpack—or at least what I thought was my backpack. When I returned I discovered the unbelievable truth. I had been keeping careful vigil over a garbage can that, from a distance, had doubled for the bulky pack. My backpack, along with my clothes, sleeping bag, and everything I owned in the world, was gone. All I had were the clothes on my back and $4 in my pocket—and too much pride to call home for help.

Some sympathetic hippies, fresh from the Rainbow gathering, gave me a ride to a Christian halfway house in Eugene, where I was graciously given refuge. Those kind people provided me with food, shelter, a much-needed shower, and abundant prayer. But I appreciated none of it. To my hostile, unconverted mind, Christians were weaklings; Christians were fools. I determined I would literally beg, borrow, and steal to escape their insufferable goodness and recover my coveted freedom.

I'm ashamed to admit it, but steal I did.[2] Disdaining the faded discards offered by the local Salvation Army, I spent the next few days brazenly shoplifting a brand-new backpack and its entire contents. The only article too large for me to smuggle out of a store was a sleeping bag, without which I remained, in my estimation, trapped.

As I wandered aimlessly through town, sullenly considering my options, I paused absently in front of a funeral home. Dejected, I glanced down at the sidewalk—and spotted a neatly folded $20 bill. Elated, I snatched up the bill and fairly flew down the street—and ran into a camping supply store sporting a banner that read: "Clearance—Sleeping Bags $19.95." I panhandled the tax and was back on the Interstate without so much as a thank-you to those kind Christians.

Why the $20 bill? Did it fall there by chance? Was it placed there by Providence—perhaps in response to the earnest intercession of "weak and foolish" Christians? I've never doubted it, at least not since I've happily joined their ranks. And every time I think of it, I shake my head in awe and disbelief that a pure and holy God would so graciously favor such an undeserving wretch.

Yet God cannot find it within Himself to do less. Unadulterated agapē—is compelled to be "kind to the ungrateful and wicked"; compelled to cause the "sun to rise on the evil and the good," the "rain [to fall] on the righteous and the unrighteous" (Luke 6:35; Matt. 5:45, NIV). But is it as a self-sufficient Creator, or a self-sacrificing Redeemer, that God is entitled and enabled to pour "every good and perfect gift" upon a prodigal humanity (James 1:17)?

"To the death of Christ we owe even this earthly life. The bread we eat is the purchase of His broken body. The water we drink is bought by His spilled blood. Never one, saint or sinner, eats his daily food, but he is nourished by the body and the blood of Christ" (*The Desire of Ages*, p. 660).

Sun and rain, food and drink, all that makes this life worth living come to us by way of the infinite sacrifice of the Son of God. Insensible to this, we trample the precious blood to secure what it has bought us. Yet He does not hold back, but gives Himself without reserve or partiality. It's a risky way to win our love. But He's decided we're worth that calculated risk.

And for that, He has my undying devotion.

---

[1] The Rainbow Family is a worldwide self-described "nonorganization of nonmembers" united by a shared devotion to alternative lifestyles and spirituality. They gather annually in the national forests to fellowship and pray for world peace.

[2] A practice that later landed me in a Washington jail.

Thirteen

This Is My Body

I've never been much for rituals, religious or otherwise. While some find meaning and solace in the repetition of symbolic words and gestures, I'm always left without a clue. As a kid in school, the more I placed my hand on my heart and pledged allegiance to the flag, the more meaningless it felt. As an earnest young Catholic, the more I made the sign of the cross and sincerely recited my Hail Marys and Our Fathers (the Lord's Prayer), the less sense they seemed to make.

And as a young adult convert to Seventh-day Adventism, the practical significance of the ordinances of foot washing and Communion eluded me. After all, nobody's feet were really *dirty,* so why wash them? And while I could appreciate, to some extent, that "the bread we eat is the purchase of [Christ's] broken body" and "the wine we drink is bought by His spilled blood," I couldn't fathom those microscopic wafers and thimblefuls of Welch's grape juice (*The Desire of Ages,* p. 660). Sorry to say, repetition didn't improve my comprehension.

One Communion Sabbath last year, I decided I was tired of being such a thickheaded philistine. As the elders asked the blessing for the bread, I asked the Lord, "What's my problem? Why can't I seem to feel engaged and connected with these divinely ordained symbols? I really do appreciate what they represent, so why don't I feel more involved as I partake?"

Absorbed in my private frustration, I vaguely heard the pastor invite the congregation to share their praise and prayer requests. Vern, a longtime elder, spoke first. "I just want to thank the Lord for bearing with me, for never giving up on me." Then he confided, with emotion, "And I'm so grateful my brother, Gene, has come back to the Lord and married a wonderful woman."

Gene, who had crept in unnoticed with his new bride, stood and blurted, to Vern's surprise, "I thank God too for not giving up on me, and for slapping me upside the head when I needed it!"

Affectionate laughter was followed by Debbie's grateful thanks for God's perseverance in *her* life; JoAnn's appreciation for prayers and encouragement in behalf of her beloved prison ministry; Jesse James's request for prayer for those "that go down to the sea in ships" (Ps. 107:23), as he was preparing to do off the Alaskan coast.

As Pastor John concluded with the familiar words "This is my body given for you; do this in remembrance of me" (Luke 22:19, NIV), my Communion mental block seemed to shift. I sensed the Lord sweeping His hand across that living sanctuary and asking me, "Do you understand now what this means? Look around you— *this* is My body. These brothers and sisters whom you so easily judge and take for granted; who suffer and seek alongside you; who struggle and fail and struggle again, as you do—*these* are My body. And because they are My body, they're *your* body, also."

My body, *my* blood, my kindred spirits in Christ. Pretty heavy stuff for a habitual loner, a devoted individualist. But it's become the only context in which Communion carries any meaning for me.

As I'm reconciled to my God by the sacrifice of my Savior, I can't help being reconciled to His church. The bread and the wine, no longer a sterile, private ceremony between my soul and my Savior, have become the corporate celebration of reconciliation He's always meant them to be. The foot washing, an illustration of the power He's granted believers to refresh one another spiritually; to identify with and lift one another's burdens; even to help cleanse one another from sin, through the ministries of Christlike empathy and intercessory prayer.

There's a mystery here that I have not, by any means, fully apprehended. A mystery of unity that is incomprehensible to the natural mind; foreign, at best, to my individualistic Western mind. Mysteriously but vitally, I'm connected to this improbable body of believers; vitally connected, also, to brothers and sisters I have not yet known, who are separated from me by distance and even death. And I'm intrigued by an unfamiliar yearning to know them all; to hear their stories; to play a part, however small, in bringing this disparate, displaced body together.

I yearn to see the body of Christ made whole.

Fourteen

Meanwhile, Back at the Ranch . . .

It's been a quiet winter in Chloride, Arizona.* As usual, the Immortal Gunfighters, Chloride's Wild West reenactors, have been hamming it up at Cyanide Springs, their rustic Main Street replica. Four new pedigreed heifers from Casper, Wyoming, can be seen kicking up their heels at the fledgling 2-Star-M Rodeo Ranch. And the Chloride Post Office, circa 1920, will soon emerge, sleek and squeaky clean, from its first-ever face-lift. Personally, I'm not looking forward to the generic new look.

The Chamber of Commerce continues to grieve the recent demise of its dearly beloved highway sign—it's a long story, but blame it on ADOT ordinance ARS 28-7906 and Lady Bird Johnson's highway beautification project. The wake and the free potluck were a huge success, however, and the chamber has found some consolation in its brisk sales of commemorative PVC crosses, which (at $5 a pop) adorn the site of the fallen sign.

Things have been pretty quiet on the home front. Y2K came and passed without so much as a whimper. In fact, our nine hens, who had been noncompliant, non-egg-laying slackers since early October, suddenly reconsidered and sprang into egg-laying compliance with the arrival of the new millennium. New Year's morning brought a single flawless brown egg and the assurance that all the chicken feed would once again be turned into Spanish omelets.

Shortly before Christmas, Jenny's Holland lop, Buttercup, fell for a handsome young buck at the Wild Rose Ranch and Rabbitry. Following a brief explosive courtship and whirlwind honeymoon, the exhausted new bride was chauffeured home. But as the girls and I pulled up the drive, our heads filled with visions of furry little balls of new life, we were greeted by a shockingly different reality.

Just ahead of us and about 10 feet from her open cage lay the limp, unnaturally sprawled form of Cookie, Becky's white-and-cinnamon Holland lop. As we tried to comprehend how such a thing could happen, up raced our neighbors' escaped German shepherd, Elsa. Then we knew. Able to clear five-foot fences in a single bound and open doors with her paws, Elsa was obviously the panting perpetrator. Becky burst into sobs at the thought.

Her grief was intense. But when you're 8 years old and eager to live and love again, time and the winsome charms of a cuddly new ball of fluff have a way of bringing sweet forgetfulness. Our neighbors bought Becky a little Dutch doe to take Cookie's place, and Becky has fallen head over heels for Rose.

Our hearts are warmed by our daughters' love of animals and all things created. All winter we've watched them stir buckets of mud and haul armloads of rocks. We've listened to animated accounts of visiting chipmunks and skittering quail. We've struggled to supply satisfactory answers to urgent questions about rabbits and cows, death and life—questions that range from the easy ("Do cows have teeth?") to the complex ("Why did God let Elsa kill my rabbit?") to the classic and always intimidating ("How do babies get born?"). (The "get born" part we can deal with; it's explaining the conception part that makes us nervous.)

And so the winter has passed in our neck of the woods. This spring we'll see what the garden can do after gathering life and richness from its winter blanket of alfalfa, earthworm castings, and local manure. We'll see how production improves when we add a new crop of pullets to our flock of aging biddies. We'll see if I'm as brave as I think I am when 20,000 Italian honeybees arrive in the mail, eager to be installed into their newly assembled hives.

In this season of new beginnings, we'll see what the Lord has in store for us in this offbeat little community called Chloride; in this unique and unpredictable place we call home. Dorothy had it right when she told Auntie Em there's no place like it. Be it ever so common, quirky (and sometimes kitschy), there's no place on earth like home.

---

* May Garrison Keillor forgive me for this bit of semiplagiarism.

Innocence Lost—Righteousness Found!

*S*ummer, and the desert is crawling with all things buggy. Grasshoppers flit among the overflowing zucchini plants; stink bugs waddle along rocky paths. The rising sun casts its brilliance on a crazy quilt of colorful moths and June bugs congregated around the darkened porch light. Drowsing and still, they know not the time of their visitation—for Jenny, Tireless Stalker of Bugs and All Things Creeping, is on the prowl for fresh victims.

Jenny doesn't think of them as victims, of course. Our 6-year-old regards her bewildered captives as fortunate pets who have transcended dull subsistence for a better life. Just now she gently plops Angela and Elizabeth, twin June bugs, into their new home, a roomy plastic container landscaped with red wash sand, glittering quartz, and creosote bouquets.

"Here's your water," she coos, offering a brimming jam jar lid. "And this is your food," she bids solicitously, poking a weedy sprig at Angela's mandibles.

"Here's the living room, bedroom, and bathroom—and don't forget to use your litter box!" she admonishes, directing the clueless Elizabeth to a square inch of napkin. Then, suddenly overwhelmed with the pure joy of it all, Jenny turns toward me and gushes, "Look, Mom, I'm potty-training my June bugs!"

And, overwhelmed with the pure joy of watching her perfect, innocent play, I can only gush back, "Yes, honey, you're sure taking good care of your little pets."

Anyone who's been there knows the unabashed pride that threatens to burst a parent wide open at such moments—a grateful pride at being able to provide for and share in the innocent pleasure of our little ones. And every devoted parent knows what burns just back of that swelling pride—a fierce determination to protect our children's purity, joy, and innocence from a world just dying to steal it away.

Since sin began, this world has fed voraciously on innocence; has fattened itself on the spent virtue of each new generation. As F. Scott Fitzgerald, whose life is a study in dissipated youth, phrased it: "Just as a cooling pot gives off heat, so all through youth and ado-lescence we give off calories of virtue." And those who have grown cold and void "stand around and literally *warm themselves*" at our expense.*

Sadly, none of us can completely disavow participa-tion in this sordid business. None can claim that the urge to shield our children from this exploitation of their ingenuousness springs strictly from our experi-ence as innocent victims. The unfortunate truth is that we know how the system works because we've partici-pated in it. Fortified with the appropriate justification, we have warmed ourselves at another's fading fire; we have traded virtue for gain. And we've all been made colder and poorer in the process.

Tragically, there is no return road to innocence. Innocence lost is lost forever, for it is a fragile, finite thing. Once it is spent it can't be regained; and as it is spent, we are changed. Eyes have been opened to the darker possibilities inherent in human nature, includ-ing our own. Such awakenings inevitably transform, making us tired, disillusioned, and exceedingly careful.

But here is a miracle: Lost innocence has been replaced by a greater force for good—by righteousness, even the righteousness of Christ. Jesus has transcended innocence to forge a new, spiritually mature dynamic— the righteousness of God perfected in human flesh.

Taking upon Him "the infirmities of degenerate humanity," "with all its liabilities," Christ "perfected [a righteous character] by a life of constant resistance of evil" (*The Desire of Ages,* p. 117; *The Acts of the Apostles,* p. 531). By a daily denial of self according to the principle of the cross, "Not my will, but thine be done," Jesus set humanity free from its helpless addiction to evil (Luke 22:42). And this dynamic, overcoming righteousness He imparts to all who will accept it by faith.

By faith, the innocent may have strength and discernment to "stand against the wiles of the devil" (Eph. 6:11). The fallen may be granted another chance to value and protect the fragile gifts of wonder, joy, and virtue. The unwillingly exploited, the ignorantly unappreciative and disobedient, all may receive righteousness to meet every need.

By faith, all who have been so blessed may cooperate with Christ in the larger work of redemption, and cry out for love of a tired and disillusioned world: "Shower, O heavens, from above, and let the skies rain down righteousness" (Isa. 45:8, RSV).

---

* F. Scott Fitzgerald, *This Side of Paradise,* p. 258.

Sixteen

The Tyranny of "Cool"

When my sisters and I were young, we didn't drift off to dreamland with the exploits of David and Goliath or the brave Queen Esther ringing in our ears. In the absence of a scriptural orientation, we slipped off to meet the sandman with visions of the Snow Queen and the Ugly Duckling floating through our dreamy heads. And though I've since forgotten how Gerda got to the Snow Queen's palace, and just what Chickabiddy Shortshanks said to the Ugly Duckling, I can still remember the delightful details of my favorite Hans Christian Andersen classic, "The Emperor's New Clothes."

You remember the story: Two traveling con men offer to weave for a vain, foppish emperor a set of clothes so fine and so delicate that anyone who is either "unfit for his office or stupid" is unable to see them. Then stashing the cash and expensive materials, the men proceed to energetically weave on their looms nothing at all, while duping the entire city into denying the evidence of their senses and agreeing that the nonexistent cloth on the empty looms is the most exquisite they've ever seen. Indeed, the emperor, rather than expose his apparent lack of savoir-faire, opts instead to publicly expose his royal self as he removes his clothes, dons his "elegant new suit," and parades naked through the streets.

Such is the tremendous power of groupthink on a

vulnerable ego. Such is the irresistible influence exerted by a decadent popular culture on those who crave the praise of their peers more than they value truth and self-respect. Such is the tyranny of "cool."

We are daily overshadowed by the tyranny of cool. Our senses and sensibilities are bombarded with its unreasonable and degrading demands to wear it or watch it, sip it or smoke it, buy it off the newsstand or surreptitiously glance at it in the express lane. Whether we realize it or not, we are ceaselessly stalked by a seductive, tyrannical conspiracy of cool.

By conspiracy of cool, I'm not referring primarily to the boardroom intrigues of the tobacco, alcohol, and entertainment industries. These producers and purveyors of coolness will be held accountable for their participation in the degradation and destruction of the human race. Yet they and their myriad counterparts remain the pimps and pawns of a greater conspiracy of cool, a conspiracy of which most of them are manifestly ignorant.

Paul discloses the nature of this conspiracy as he cautions: "For our struggle is not against flesh and blood, but against the rulers, against the authorities, against the powers of this dark world and against the spiritual forces of evil in the heavenly realms" (Eph. 6:12, NIV).

And my favorite inspirational writer, Ellen White, reveals its eminently successful strategy: "Through the medium of influence, taking advantage of the action of mind on mind, [Satan] prevailed on Adam to sin. Thus at its very source human nature was corrupted. And ever since then sin has continued its hateful work, reaching from mind to mind" (*Review and Herald*, Apr. 16, 1901).

Surely "our struggle is *not* against flesh and blood."
It's against a quintessential con artist who promises to
weave for us the most gorgeous apparel, then leaves us
naked in the street. It's against a consummate manipu-
lator who understands far better than we the complexi-
ties of the human mind, and the power that one mind,
or many minds under his influence, can exert over another—through intimidation, enticement, or an every-
body's-doing-it mandate.

And what is the ultimate target of this sophisticated
satanic onslaught? The delicate, developing minds and
hearts of our children, of course. Which is why, in con-
tradiction to our culture, my husband and I are committed to imitating "the conditions chosen by the
infinite Father" for His Son's impressionable childhood—"a secluded home . . . sustained by honest, self-
respecting labor; a life of simplicity; daily conflict with
difficulty and hardship; self-sacrifice, economy, and
patient, gladsome service; the hour of study at His
mother's side, with the open scroll of Scripture; the
quiet of dawn or twilight in the green valley; the holy
ministries of nature; the study of creation and provi-
dence; and the soul's communion with God" (*The
Ministry of Healing*, pp. 365, 366).

This is the simple yet elegant life my husband and I
have chosen for our girls. Though quaint and austere
by today's standards, we believe it's the most nourishing soil in which to plant and cultivate the characters
they'll need to say *no* to the pervasive tyranny of cool,
and *yes* to God's more abundant life. And though we
still have a lot to learn about this life, so far in our
home it looks like this.

We're hopelessly politically incorrect. In this age of

the mythical supermom who purportedly has it all, successfully juggling children and career, community activism and church involvement, I'm an uncooperative, underachieving dropout. Lacking the energy and ambition to have it all, I've settled for the slow but sweet rewards that come from giving my all to my children, because I don't think they're going to make it through this world and into the kingdom of God any other way.

While staying home with my kids isn't a magic potion, I believe it affords the only realistic opportunity for me to consistently participate in and direct their development. It firmly attaches their dependence and affections to me, not to their peers or another caregiver. It lets them know that I consider them the most important career I could ever engage in. And it's actually (though sometimes barely) affordable, since we've simplified our lifestyle and significantly curbed our consumptive habits.

We're vitally connected to the community of faith. It's been suggested that "it takes a village" to raise a child. Certainly that's true if the "village" understands from Scripture what is for the child's eternal good and supports the values, aims, and just authority of the parents. Sadly, we don't believe this to be the case with our culture. So for us, the village is the church. Though our remote location makes it somewhat of a challenge, we do our best to maintain a strong connection with our local church family. We want our children to regard it as a loving and supportive extension of our own family, a place and a people they'll continue to call their own as they grow older.

We're training them up in the way they should go, so when they're old they won't depart from it. Some have understood Proverbs 22:6 to mean that when children are faithfully trained in the way that is true and best, they'll remain loyal to it when they are grown. Others have understood the text to stress that when children's temperament and genetic makeup—their "way"—are understood and sensitively taken into account, they'll choose to remain true to their training. We believe the truth to be a happy marriage of the two, and that's why we've chosen to home-school.

With home schooling we have the flexibility to tailor our children's educational programs to fit their interests and capabilities. We can allow them to explore and mature at their own pace in a low-key, nonthreatening, noncompetitive environment. We can shield them from unhealthy influences and relationships while we help them establish their self-worth in Christ. We can teach them to be creative, independent thinkers, not mere reflectors of others' thoughts. And we can savor the learning process right along with them.

We're asking "the beasts . . . the birds of the air . . . [and] the plants of the earth" to teach us about our God (Job 12:7, 8, RSV). Our stony, sun-drenched valleys aren't green, but they're quiet and secluded, and the "ministries of nature" are just as holy here as in more fertile landscapes. The sky is huge and clean; the stars on a summer's night are breathtakingly bright and beyond counting. The unfenced hills invite our children to run and explore, to stretch their legs and their minds. The silky wash sand, desert marigolds, and tiny scrub oak acorns are the raw material of their imaginative play. All of this together attracts our children's minds away from the trendy and artificial to the unaffected, awesome beauty of nature, and binds their hearts to nature's God.

We're carefully guarding our senses, because they are the avenues to our souls. Country living isn't the automatic hedge against undesirable influences it once was. We can electronically import the same audio, video, and online entertainment and information available to our urban and suburban counterparts. So even out here in the sticks, we must constantly guard against the intrusion of any influence that would nullify our best efforts to worldproof our kids—because by beholding we become changed, for better or for worse.

We're strengthening our minds by building up our bodies. It's a well-documented fact that a vital, sympathetic relationship exists between the mind and the body. In order to strengthen one, we must strengthen the other, that the whole person may be built up for good. Tired, unhealthy children find it far more difficult to discern and resist temptation than those who are rested and invigorated. They're more likely to crave the momentary boost of a strong chemical, sensual, visual, or auditory stimulus, greatly increasing their susceptibility to drug use and junk food cravings, immorality, and unhealthy viewing and listening habits.

Because of this, we've decided that one of the most important ways we can build up our children's minds is to help them have strong, healthy bodies. So we base our philosophy of health on the eight natural remedies of pure air, sunlight, temperance, rest, exercise, proper diet, the use of water, and trust in divine power (*The Ministry of Healing,* p. 127). We maintain a simple nondairy, low-fat, sugar-free vegetarian diet—emphasizing all the good things we get to eat, not all the goodies we "sacrificially" deny ourselves.

We're "talkin' 'bout our generation." When I was a
teenager, I reveled in my rebellious, youth-worshiping
culture. A good soldier in the ranks of mindless mimicry,
I bought the lies and obediently chanted the anthems of
my heroes. I've since concluded that the so-called generation gap is largely a creation of the fashion and entertainment industries' imaginations—another example of
the devil's divide-and-conquer strategy, made eminently
successful by parental ignorance and disinterest.

Though my husband and I recognize that basic differences exist between us and our children, in Christ
there is much more that brings us together than sepa-
rates us. We believe togetherness is what it's all
about—because whoever spends the most time with our
children wins. If we don't disciple them, popular culture
and their misinformed peers will. So we plan our lives
around spending time with our kids, because when it's
all over, we hope to be the generation that greets our
Lord in the air *together.*

As our daughters bounce from one intriguing adven-
ture to the next, it's evident that so far they're satisfied
with our simple but full life together. They have questions, which we welcome, and complaints, which we
consider. But their thoughts, goals, and affections are
basically in harmony with ours. True, they're still young,
and they've been largely shielded from the tantalizing
perversion of their culture. They haven't yet been confronted with the full force of peer pressure. Soon enough
their times of severe testing will come, when they'll be
forced to conspicuously stand for truth and self-respect
or join with the crowd in proclaiming the emperor's new
clothes the most exquisite they've ever seen.

So we prepare them as best we can, guiding them

through the small but crucial decisions of childhood. We pray daily for their thorough conversion and for our own completely consecrated examples. We study their ways and the Lord's way, that we may understand how to cultivate within them strong, vibrant characters with the capacity for discernment and independent thought. We give them ourselves in Christ so that they may find their unshakable identity in Him, through us.

And we rest in the promise of One who is greater than all the satanic legions of the conspiracy of cool. "Can the prey be taken from the mighty, or the captives of a tyrant be rescued? Surely, thus says the Lord: 'Even the captives of the mighty shall be taken, and the prey of the tyrant be rescued, for I will contend with those who contend with you, and I will save your children'" (Isa. 49:24, 25, RSV)—even from the pervasive tyranny of cool.

Seventeen

You Say "Tomato" . . .

. . . and I say "succulent queen of the nightshades." You say "potato"—well, you get the idea. There's more than one way to relate to a vegetable.

And there's more than one way to relate to a symphony. My husband, Don, has been known to shrug, "I guess that Beethoven guy wrote some decent stuff; but that fifth is too busy for me."

And I've been known to gasp in response, "'Busy'? Honey, that's not *busy*—that's passion, sensitivity, the agony and the ecstasy of the human spirit! Complex, yes, but *busy?*" We are, in a word, different.

We listen differently and hear differently; eat our tomatoes and potatoes differently. And, not least, we remember differently—in that, generally speaking, Don doesn't. If it isn't engraved on the insides of his eyelids or grafted onto his body, my preoccupied husband will forget it. I, on the other hand, forget nothing. (Except those pesky, pervasive numbers— telephone, checking account, Social Security, and the quantity of zeroes attached to the ends of large figures. Hey, they're just zeros—how important can they be?)

A recent example: I pick up the phone on a Friday in January and am greeted by that refrain whose appeal wanes with each passing year, "Happy Birthday to you . . ." My dad and stepmom, Jeanne, interrupt their duet to ask, "So, does the birthday girl have anything special planned for today?"

"Special? Uh, no," I stammer. "I haven't really thought about it. In fact, I forgot it was my birthday." I'm allowed to forget this.

"You forgot?" they echo in disbelief. "Hasn't anyone reminded you yet?" It is now midmorning.

"No. . . . I guess *everyone else* forgot too." The phrase "everyone else" is delivered with the pained resignation and restrained sarcasm to which one so aggrieved is entitled—and refers, of course, to my husband, who is *not* allowed to forget.

It takes a few days, but we work out this minor wrinkle—just in time for our next ill-fated jaunt down Memory Lapse Lane.

As the four of us rattle off in our old flatbed to fetch some free lumber from my dad, I ask the all-important question, "Did you remember to get gas in town today?" ("Town" meaning Kingman; we have no gas station in Chloride.)

Without consulting the gauge, which hasn't worked since we've owned the truck, Don casually replies, "No, but I think we're all right."

Filled with a sense of foreboding, I persist, "Don't you think we should fill it up in Dolan Springs?"

"Oh, we could put a few gallons in," he concedes nonchalantly. But two hours later, with our mission accomplished, neither of us remembers the gas. Back on the highway we clatter, 300 board feet of redwood richer, when suddenly we sense a faint lurch, a sputter, and the sound of four wheels rolling quietly into the sunset.

"Oh no," groans my husband. "We forgot to get gas!"

Silently I take exception to his use of the word *we*.

He, after all, forgot the gas *first*. Since when am *I* implicated in this fiasco?

"What about the gas can, Daddy?" pipes Becky. "Isn't there any gas in it?"

"I don't have the gas can," answers Daddy.

"Where is it?" asks Jenny.

"Somebody stole it," Daddy replies, with a faintly hunted look.

"Oh, I don't *think* so—what's the rest of the story?" I goad.

"Somebody *did* steal it from Isaac's transmission shop," asserts Dad, "where I forgot it."

So we lock up the truck and start the long hike home. Thank the Lord we're soon helped by a kind Samaritan who crams us into his Toyota pickup and blasts us to our doorstep at 80 miles per hour. While our new friend assures my husband of the many advantages of becoming an Amway distributor, I march into the house and inflict my frustrations on the dirty dishes.

Somewhere into the flatware I'm surprised by the faintest giggle roaming around my insides. By the time I get to the pots and pans I'm shaking with laughter. What a life! What a husband! But he's mine—my own absentminded, sweet-natured gift from God. And I am his, prissy self-righteousness and all.

Different, flawed, one in Christ. We repent and forgive, accept each other in the Beloved, and face the world together.

In Whom Is No Guile

I like animals. I like their honesty. I like the way they make it exuberantly, unmistakably clear when they like you, and snub you into oblivion when they don't. I envy their emotional freedom and spontaneity as I feel them purr with contentment, watch them kick up their heels for joy, or hear them howl in abject mourning.

Animals couldn't care less about the subtleties of social subterfuge. You'll never catch them browsing the self-help section for books with names like *Winning Through Manipulation;* never find them attending seminars titled "The Power of Pretense—Awakening the Artful Dodger Within."[1] Except for the occasional bad seed—such as the purring tabby who affectionately rubs your leg, then shreds your outstretched hand and dashes to the top of her cat tree, glaring triumphantly as she goes[2]—animals are a pretty straightforward, transparent bunch.

Not so people. As a species we're a guarded, insincere lot. By the time we reach adulthood we've become adept at saying yes when we mean no; at smiling serenely when we feel like dying of sorrow; at professing "I can't" when we lack the courage to admit "I won't." Sandwiched between external pressures to conform and produce and the internal dictates of pride and ambition, we conclude that protective pretension is better than honest vulnerability. And we wonder why nobody understands us.

No wonder Jesus expressed astonishment upon meeting the candid Nathanael, whom He described as "an Israelite indeed, in whom is no guile" (John 1:47). Even among the people of God, in a comparatively unsophisticated culture, a truly artless, authentic character was a rare find. How much more today, in a popular culture that vaunts style above substance; in a religious climate that often contents itself with "a form of godliness, [while] denying the power thereof" (2 Tim. 3:5).

Yet it is smack in the swirling center of this culture of insincerity that God is even now, quietly, committedly, cultivating a people about whom it may be said, "In their mouth [is] found no guile: for they are without fault before the throne of God" (Rev. 14:5).

The longer I'm a Christian, the more convinced I am that the most revulsive, most insidious characteristic of sin is not its power to make us smoke and drink and live promiscuously. The black heart of sin is its fantastic power to deceive—to make us lie to ourselves and to each other about who we are and why we do what we do; to twist us every which way but straight until we don't even know the simple truth of who we are in Christ. Apparently this quality of deception is so intrinsic to sin that if we are finally separated from it, we are pronounced without fault before God's judgment seat.

Though it is outside the realm of our experience, God's Word assures us that this separation from deception will happen. Christ, our great high priest, will succeed in completely liberating a people from the subtle, pervasive power of guile. He will succeed in revealing hidden weaknesses and motives to eyes that are willing to see. He will succeed in establishing ultimate honesty in hearts that have decided there is nothing to be lost by abandoning pretense, and everything of value to be gained.

This is the experience I covet—though I can never perceive myself to have attained it, lest my last state of deception be more wretched than the first. "But I press on to take hold of that for which Christ Jesus took hold of me" (Phil. 3:12, NIV). I press on to find my identity and security in Him, so I'll no longer feel the need to rationalize and pretend. I press on to become "as transparent as the sunlight," relinquishing the "right" to cherish and indulge a secret self (*Thoughts From the Mount of Blessing*, p. 68).

I press on to be part of an end-time body of believers that is determined to be found without guile in Christ, that His character of truth may finally be vindicated in His people.

---

[1] These are fictional titles that, these days, may as well be factual.

[2] Description based on combat experience with Grandpa Greenfield's Baby Lady, who invariably sent visiting grandchildren home with fresh scars and a thirst for revenge.

Nineteen

The Fullness of the Time

For all their winsome, endearing young charms, babies are unpredictable, often contrary creatures. Resisting their exhausted parents' best efforts to shepherd them into some semblance of a schedule, they noisily demand food when they feel like it; nap when, where, and if they feel like it; and feign a mysterious ailment called "colic" when they feel like raising a little Cain. All of which, come to think of it, is consistent with their noisy, unpredictable entrance into this world—at the precise moment they feel like it.

Each December, however, the Christian world celebrates the birth of a Baby who broke rank with His unpredictable peers and was born right on schedule. Scripture tells us that "when the fulness of the time was come, God sent forth his Son, made of a woman" (Gal. 4:4).

That is, at the time foreknown and foretold by God, the infant Jesus opened innocent eyes and gazed into His mother's tired, radiant face as she gathered Him into her open arms.

Two thousand years later we yearn to fill our eyes with the beauty and brilliance of His radiant face as He returns in glory to gather His people to Himself. Yet when we inquire as to why our "blessed hope" has not yet been realized, we're often told not to worry—Jesus came on time the first time and, we're assured, He will come on time the second time. Personally, I find the assurance not at all comforting, but intensely frustrating.

The longer I walk with God, the more my perception of Him changes. My earliest conception of God was that of benevolent dictator, a loving but absolute authority figure whose sovereign will could not be broken, either in terms of time or circumstance. I have since come to view Him in more democratic terms, as a leader whose sovereign will continually interacts with, and is affected by, our exercise of free choice—within the limits of ultimate boundaries, of course.

The downside of all this freedom is that it's possible to frustrate, and even delay, the outworking of God's will. Scripture is replete with examples. Motivated by unbelief, Abraham "helped" God fulfill His promise of a son, and the consequences haunt us to this day. On the borders of the Promised Land, blinded by pride and unbelief, Israel delayed their entrance an unscheduled 40 years, grieving and dishonoring God in the process (see *Patriarchs and Prophets*, p. 464). In the years following, God's people frustrated His will more often than not, ultimately betraying and nullifying His purpose for their national existence.

The good news is that we can choose to positively influence outcomes by humbly yet confidently participating in the divine decision-making process. When God threatened to annihilate Israel during the golden calf debacle, Moses discerned in the threat an invitation to change God's mind (*ibid.*, pp. 318, 319; Ex. 32:7-14). When God confided in His friend Abraham that Sodom had exhausted its probationary opportunities, Abraham received the confidence as an encouragement to influence the destiny of that wicked city (*ibid.*, pp. 139, 140;

Gen. 18:16-33). When Daniel understood that the 70 years of Jerusalem's captivity, as prophesied by Jeremiah, were approaching their fulfillment, he didn't passively rest in the assurance of a foregone conclusion. He united his will with God's and "pleaded with him in prayer and petition, in fasting, and in sackcloth and ashes"—for the forgiveness and deliverance that had already been promised (Dan. 9:2, 3, NIV; Jer. 25:1-14).

Are there any exceptions here? Is there any aspect of God's dealings with humanity from which our participation has been precluded? To my knowledge, there have been two—the objective facts of Creation and redemption. No thanks to us, God created the world and wrought out redemption for the world. But insofar as we subjectively interact with these facts, we bear the responsibility and privilege of influencing eternal outcomes.

The process has been progressive. The faith and unbelief of each generation builds upon and compounds that which has come before. The cup fills, the harvest ripens, the intensity builds to fever pitch as the church and the world surge toward the consummation of history and their hearts' desires. Though the Father foreknows when that consummation will be, He has not predetermined it. Within the limits of divinely set boundaries, the Lord permits us to establish the fullness of our time.

Twenty

Simple Gifts

On a blistering Wednesday last summer a few country mice got the itch to see how it fared with their big city cousins. So the Kay clan packed up the old brown wagon (station wagon, that is), waved goodbye to their Chloride compatriots, and headed up the highway to rub shoulders with their sleek urban counterparts in the big city of Las Vegas.

With my husband, Don, doing a scrap metal job in the area, we decided to meet at the Motel 6 just off The Strip and spend the evening visiting the sights. Always one to shy away from cities, especially flashy ones, I'd convinced myself that I'd been too much of a stick-in-the-mud; that I ought to let the kids branch out and see a few things. So it was that we were all surprised to find ourselves cradled in the very lap of luxurious glitz on a sultry summer evening.

After a cooling swim, we ventured out. First stop, the Treasure Island buffet. As we navigated our way through a labyrinth of furiously ringing slot machines, Becky asked, wide-eyed, "What are all these people doing, Mom?"

"They're gambling, honey," I replied.

Not at all enlightened, she persisted, "What's gambling?"

Tempted to dismiss the practice with a pastor friend's description, "Gambling is throwing your money down a rathole," I instead explained the rationale. Wonderingly our daughters gazed at the rhythmically ratcheting arms and vacant eyes and drew their own conclusions.

Dinner dispatched with, back we trudged through the clanging casino to the lush, tropical landscape of The Mirage, where the girls were duly impressed by the throbbing pyrotechnics of the simulated volcano. Then back up The Strip, under the flashing marquees, through the churning cacophony, past the sinuous stretch limos with their fully stocked bars, and the endless parade of taxis bearing too many signboards of showgirls baring far too much. Back to Treasure Island for the pirate fight, just in time to be engulfed in a crush of smoking, sweating, expectant humanity.

It was about then that a line from *Pilgrim's Progress* bobbed to my consciousness—a question Evangelist put to Christian when he had been induced by Wordly Wiseman to wander from the way: "What dost thou here, Christian?" Wincing at the personal application, I, like Christian, "knew not what to answer." I could only echo the question "What were we thinking of when we brought our children to this place?"

Thursday morning dawned hotter than ever. Creeping through traffic that intensified the 111-degree heat and thrust it fiercely through our open windows,* we doused ourselves with bottled water and turned our thoughts toward home. The gleaming hotels and casinos impassively eyed our departure—if a few simple, uncouth country mice chose to scamper back to the open fields, it was a matter of utmost indifference to them.

I would be less than honest if I said that a place like Vegas holds no attraction for me. I've never cared about gambling; that's not my weakness. But I feel the pull of the beauty all that gaming money can buy—the graceful fountains and pools; elaborate saltwater aquariums and exotic animal collections; the lush, gorgeous landscapes and impressive architecture. Yet even as I look and admire I can't forget that behind those luxurious facades coils a deadly, lying beast that takes no prisoners—only human sacrifices.

So I'm content in my austere desert. Content to watch my children grow tanned and strong in the afternoon sun. Content to gaze at the uncluttered sky and listen to the unbroken silence. Content with God's simple, character-building gifts—hard, satisfying work; the lessons of the garden; the challenges of family life; the rugged, reassuring contours of the ancient mountains.

I'm content to find my joy and fulfillment in God's simplest and most profound Gift—a common, unassuming Man who shunned luxury and display. As I watch the sun set behind a bank of brilliant red clouds, I tell Him my heart's desire:

"Nearer, still nearer, Lord, to be Thine;
Sin, with its follies, I gladly resign,
All of its pleasures, pomp and its pride;
Give me but Jesus, my Lord crucified."

---

* Don't feel too sorry for us. We could get the air-conditioner fixed if we wanted to spend the money.

Twenty-one

Blessed Are the . . . Nice?

"And seeing the multitudes, he went up into a mountain: and when he was set, his disciples came unto him: and he opened his mouth, and taught them, saying, Blessed are the nice" (Matt. 5:1-3, Nicely Revised King James Version).

Wait a minute. I guess it doesn't quite say that. But surely it's in here somewhere. Maybe this is it. "He hath shewed thee, O man, what is good; and what doth the Lord require of thee, but to do justly, and to love mercy, and to be really nice to everyone you meet" (Micah 6:8, Nicely Revised King James Version).

Wait! That's not right either. I could have sworn that *somewhere* the Lord says *something* about being *nice.* But it's just not there. How could I have been so wrong?

After all, if anyone knows niceness, it's me. At the moment of my conception legions of perky little niceness genes sweetly but firmly muscled their way into the middle of each unfolding cell. When I popped into this world, all that pent-up niceness exploded into action—the first act of my life was to help the nurses tidy up the delivery room; my first words to my mother were "I wouldn't have come if I'd known it would put you to so much trouble."

Niceness—accommodation, agreeableness, inoffensiveness—we go way back. And the best part is that all this innate niceness made becoming a Christian no trouble at all—I just brought all that good stuff along with me.

Pretty sickening, isn't it? The question is: Can such deeply entrenched, congenital niceness be cured? Can an insufferably nice person *ever* be made to see that habitual niceness is *not* a fruit of the spirit, not the standard of righteousness; not real, honest, or even healthy?

Thankfully, we can. Our flexible, creative Savior has a thousand ways to open the eyes of even the most stalwart devotee. My moments of truth have especially come in the context of parenthood.

I've found, through hard experience, what wild, woolly, sinful little children do to nice, sweet mothers and fathers. They eat them for lunch. They eat them for lunch, and they stash the crumbs in a shoebox under their beds for later. Our strong-willed firstborn has especially taught me that if I would act in her best eternal and temporal interest, I'll jettison the whole helpless concept of niceness. I'll lose my fear of that unpleasant word *no* and in the spirit of true kindness and mercy, learn to practice it confidently and redemptively.

Why is it so hard for some of us? What are we afraid will happen when we trade the aura of nice for the finality of *no?* Are we afraid our children will think we're mean and stop liking us? afraid our church family will label us selfish and disloyal? afraid our coworkers will find us unfriendly and our bosses will think we're wimpy and uncooperative? But what would *really* happen if we stopped wearing ourselves out giving people what they want, and cultivated instead the courage and insight necessary to give them what they truly need in Christ? Maybe something wonderful and revolutionary.

Jesus, who is love incarnate, gave Himself unreservedly for the redemption of the human race. But the One who best understands our unconsciously egocentric, manipulative core never gave Himself gratuitously. He never sacrificed His energies and affections, His gifts and abilities on the altar of exploitation, even for a seemingly noble cause. Jesus was too good to be nice.

It's still true—nice guys and girls *do* finish last. We spend our energies earning the approbation that never seems to satisfy. We spend our identities anticipating and fulfilling the expectations of others. In the end, the kingdom of God suffers because of our well-intentioned but ineffectual imitation of Christ.

Niceness, accommodation, conformity, are conceived in a spirit of fear, obligation, and pride. They can't help giving birth to bondage. Meekness, mercy, goodness, those grand, true attributes of the character of Christ, spring from the spirit of agapē love and give birth to freedom and eternal blessings. It's what our families, our churches, and our world really need to taste and see—an accurate, palpable expression of the living Christ.

The Good Life

*E*conomy Remains Strong" trumpeted the headlines, but as far as my husband and I could tell, the patient was anemic and fast becoming comatose. As Asia slid deeper and deeper into recession, it inexorably dragged the scrap metal market down with it. Every week our hearts sank with the sinking price of aluminum, copper, and brass. Don's flatbed returned empty more and more often as suppliers chose to hang on and wait for better days.

Then in July, a breakthrough: The 500 transmission cases Don had been trying all year to pry out of Izzy at Gibraltar Transmissions had finally come through. Five hundred cases meant 14,000 pounds of aluminum ingots. And although 16 cents a pound profit paled in comparison to 26 cents the month before, for now it would pay the bills and put food on the table.

The girls and I were in a celebratory mood as we waved Don off to Vegas. "Daddy's getting scrap—now we'll have money!" Becky chirped to 4-year-old Jenny. Giddy with optimism, we fairly danced through the round of prosaic details that make up our simple, satisfying days.

After worship it was off to do chores while the temperature still hung comfortably in the 90s. (It's a dry heat, you know.) First stop, the rabbit cage.

Any naive soul who has bought into the fantasy that

rabbits are cuddly, harmless little morsels of velveteen has never made the acquaintance of Daisy. We fell for the cinnamon-colored cutie at the feed store and carted her home on the assurance that "Holland lops are the most docile of all the breeds." I'd hate to know what the other breeds are capable of. The first time we snuggled Daisy into our laps we found that beneath her fleecy charms beat the savage heart of Amazon Bunny. She grumbled and thrashed, gnashed her great teeth, and slashed us with talon-sharp claws. As time mended our wounds but not Daisy's ways, we settled on a policy of appeasement: We would provide the carrots and greens, and Daisy would get to hop around her yard and look cute.

Carrots and greens provided, we tossed the yucky kitchen scraps into the earthworm composter and the tasty scraps to the chickens. Fluffy, the cute little gray "hen" that grew up to be a big gray rooster, stiffly presided over the dispersal. Then back up to the garden we climbed, followed by our dogs, who hoped we'd drop an egg or two along the way.

And so our day passed, as we cleaned and played and cooked and read, until evening found us watering our precious few flowers and we caught the familiar rumble of an aging Ford pickup.

"Daddy's home!" the girls cheered, and they raced to greet him as he pulled up the drive. But when he emerged, his careworn face told the tale as plainly as the empty flatbed. "I never made it to Izzy's," he sighed wearily. "I spent all day trying to fix the truck.* I finally just hot-wired it and came home." And then this doleful news: "I won't be able to get with Izzy again for a month."

And so it settled upon us, that bleakness we had come to know so well. We fretted and fussed and barely heard Becky's piping voice, "Come take my training wheels off, Dad. I think I can ride without them!"

Reluctantly we broke off our commiserations. As I watered last year's Christmas tree I watched my husband run alongside our daughter's wobbly bike and give it a mighty shove; watched her face become radiant with the realization that she was free, gliding on two wheels, growing up.

I knew as I watched that somehow it would all work out. The bills would be paid. The truck would be fixed. The kids would be fed and clothed. And so it has been. Wobbly and often insecure, unused to being stripped of all that would prevent us from depending solely upon our Lord, we step gingerly into our unaccustomed freedom. Trusting in Him, growing up into Him, we're learning to savor all the more this simple life, this good life, together.

---

* Thank you, Pastor Hancock, for sticking with him through it all and being the true friend you are.

Twenty-three

Sisters! Who Needs Them?

"I wish I didn't *have* a sister!" grumped Becky from the back seat. "I wish I was an only child, like Mom's friend Michelle!"

"Mean Beck!" her sister shot back, as the two locked eyes in a fierce glaring match that was turning an already long drive home from California into a tedious clash of wills.

As I officiated from the front seat, alternately disciplining and distracting my frustrated daughters, I remembered another batch of battling siblings who verbally slugged it out on another long drive so many years ago.

"Dad, Jennie's feet are in my face again!"

"Jennifer!" Dad commanded over his shoulder, "get your feet out of Leslie's face!"

My tormentor grudgingly removed the filthy objects from my nose level and stuck them out the car window. "They're not *in* her old face," she innocently declared, then hissed in my ear, "Baby!"

Our father was not in a mood to be trifled with. "I don't want to hear this all the way to Arkansas. Now, if I have to stop this car to make you girls behave . . ." His voice trailed off. Dad hated to make threats. "Can't you just get along?"

Get along? Maybe, if I'd been trapped in a sweaty back seat with Attila the Hun, or a pack of hungry wolverines. But get along with Jennie the Terrible? Impossible! I glanced at my sister's stuck-out tongue long enough to return the favor.

From my left, our oldest sister, Debbie, scolded, "Why can't you two stop acting like children and behave more maturely?"

Like her, no doubt. Jennie and I huffed, "And who put *you* in charge of us? You're not Mom!" Resisting Debbie's big-sisterly authority was the one thing that momentarily united Jennie and me.

Sisters! Who needs them? I was sure I could get along just fine without mine. But since nobody seemed to care what I thought, and because I was the youngest, I had been plunked, sullen and protesting, smack in the middle of these two people to whom I was related against my will. And so I was destined to ride more than 3,000 torturous miles.

Late that Friday afternoon we three girls, our father, and stepmother, Faye, had rumbled out of southern California in Faye's 1963 Cadillac, determined to endure that rite of family passage known as the summer vacation. Our destination—Jonesboro, Arkansas, Faye's hometown. We deprived Westerners were to receive an initiation into the "Three H's" of the truly civilized world—Southern hospitality, hominy grits, and humidity.

And so, with Jennie's fragrant feet stuck safely out the window, we chugged up out of the smog and into the clear breezes of the Mojave Desert. Into the barren vastness we sped, until the relentless glare of sun on sand was replaced by the brilliance of the desert night sky. In silent awe we gazed at more stars than we had ever imagined existed, until the hush and the hum of the massive motor took their toll, and our sleepy eyelids slid south.

Our economical father (*cheap* was our adjective of choice) realized that bedtime was imminent, but saw no reason to waste hard-earned cash on a motel room when we could sleep in the car for free. So as we descended into the furnace heat of the Colorado River valley, it was decided we would spend the night at a riverside rest stop.

We parked among the tamarisk trees, and Dad and Faye threw down a tarp beside the car. Debbie got the front seat, Jennie the back, and I was banished to the narrow ledge below the back window. But sleep eluded us in that smothering place, so very early morning found us back on the road.

"How much farther to Arkansas?" we yawned from the back seat.

"About 1,500 miles," our stepmother replied.

"Fifteen hundred miles!" we wailed in unison. And on we cruised, through a billowing sea of sage and an endless electric blue sky, stopping along the way just long enough to fill up our gas tank and our stomachs.

Jennie and I passed the time baiting and annoying each other and thoroughly disgusting our older sister. Debbie finally withdrew from our crude company and disappeared into her corner, where she read herself into another dimension—one in which sisters, sweltering deserts, and cramped Cadillacs didn't exist.

The next morning we rolled out of rain-soaked Tucumcari, sailed through Amarillo and Oklahoma City, and finally took a break in a mangy, muggy little town somewhere in the Ozarks. As we sat sipping cold drinks in a greasy spoon, a platoon of mosquitoes droned lazily above our heads. They seemed amiable enough until a particularly malevolent one singled me out for diving practice. It buzzed and strafed my wildly bobbing head until, in exasperation, I swung with every ounce of fury my skinny 8-year-old body could muster. I don't think the mosquito felt a thing, but my drink catapulted in one direction and I flew into the other, landing flat on my back, spread-eagled, in the middle of the place.

The family thought this was the funniest thing they'd seen since we left home, and laughed themselves silly. Jennie treated me to nonstop instant replays for the rest of the trip. I just wished that Arkansas would come quickly and mercifully.

Arkansas did finally arrive, and we loved it. Our stepmother's family treated us like the royalty we most certainly were not. Faye's mother, Pearl, regaled us with dumplings, catfish, and turnips, winning our hearts with her generosity and gracious charm. Her entertaining relatives held us spellbound with tales of panthers that shrieked like women and careless children who fell into vats of lye while making lard soap. We investigated mysterious attics and explored ancient cemeteries. We swam in every muddy pond in Craighead County, playing creature from the black lagoon.

We even got along when we weren't trying not to. Although when Debbie fell in love with a boy named Michael Nutt, Jennie and I couldn't resist serenading her with the clever refrain "Debbie loves a nut; Debbie loves a nut . . ."

Too soon, our visit ended. We climbed into our faithful Cadillac and tearfully waved goodbye to our newfound Southern friends (with Debbie waving a little more tearfully than the rest of us). As we nosed the old boat toward Oklahoma, a furious thunderstorm swept into town behind us—a fitting finale to the three little thunderclouds just blowing back out.

The trip home was much the same as the trip there. The first night found us parked in a humid, chigger-infested rest stop as we assumed our designated sleeping positions. Annoyed with my inhospitable berth, I decided to mutiny. Waiting until all was quiet, I stealthily crept to the edge of my perch and fell heavily on Jennie's sleeping form. Her anguished cry pierced the night.

"I'm sorry—I didn't mean to!" I lied.

"Yes, you did! You did it on purpose! Dad!"

"If you girls don't be quiet and go to sleep . . ."

After three days of baking sun and overpriced souvenir shops, we descended into the dreaded Colorado River valley and were immediately assaulted by a smothering blanket of heat.

"How much longer?" came the panting chorus from the back seat.

"About five hours," our father replied.

"Five hours!" we groaned in unison, and settled back for the final stretch—until two extremely filthy feet appeared in my face.

"Dad, her feet are in my face *again!*"

"Jennifer!"

Sisters! Who needs them? As three girls tussled and teased in the back seat of a dusty Cadillac barreling west on Route 66—and two dirty feet waved wildly in the breeze—I didn't think I did. But the passing years have convinced me otherwise.

I've watched Jennifer grow up from a bratty big sister to a talented, graceful woman with a gift for creating beauty. I've watched her devotedly play both father and mother to her two young children when she was all they had. I've watched her bravely endure emotional hardship, including the tragic illness and loss of her oldest child. I respect and admire her immensely, and consider it a privilege to name my youngest daughter in her honor.

Our oldest sister, Debbie, forgave all our meanness and immaturity and blossomed into a beautiful, gifted woman. I've watched her organize and coordinate a thriving family business and an active household. I've watched her love her husband and her children with every ounce of her generous being.

And for the past three years I've helplessly watched something else I never dreamed I'd live to see. I have watched my sweet, gentle sister Debbie wage an unbelievably courageous war against the ravages and indignities of a destroyer called cancer; and, though her indomitable spirit cried "Live!" her enemy, at last, proved too great for her.

I said goodbye to my sister on a warm, fragrant morning in May. I wept it silently, to the sweet, melancholy crying of bagpipes, in a green suburban cemetery, in the company of family and friends. And I whispered that I would see her again, strong and beautiful, when the Lord returns to make things right.

Three sisters have grown, and one rests in the Lord. But two little ones rush to fill the gap in the cycle of life. As a little brown Nissan speeds east on Interstate 40, away from the soft ocean breezes of southern California, two young sisters squabble and scrap in the back seat, in classic sister style, trying to find out what sort of stuff the other is made of. Though they don't yet realize it, two sisters are learning to love, learning to be the special friends they will become in time; learning to need the special friendship that only a sister can provide.

Twenty-four

The Pause That Distresses

Football coach Vince Lombardi once said, "Fatigue makes cowards of us all"—including the sport's strongest men. To that astute observation I would add this corollary—the rigors of menopause can make irritable, insomniac, fatigued cowards of even the strongest women who fall into its sweaty embrace. Oh, I know—it's not a flattering depiction. It flies in the face of the carefully cultivated image of the steely-eyed, got-it-all-together goddess of the new millennium. But biology is, well, there—like Mount Everest. Wishfully denying its intractable thereness won't make it go away.

While it's true that some women cruise through this midlife passage without a hitch or a hot flash, not all are so fortunate. I've been initiated into that sisterhood of hormonally challenged souls who sail into the waters of menopause in apparently seaworthy vessels, only to find our suddenly leaky hulls listing dangerously off course. We can only shake our heads and exclaim, "What's happened to the bodies and minds we thought we knew so well?"

Sleep that once came readily flees, and, when it allows itself to be apprehended, shakes us off prematurely in a drenching sweat. Concentration that enabled us to master a thousand details abandons us to the ranks of the single-tasking. Moods that used to be (reasonably) rational and consistent could write the sequel to *Dr. Jekyll and Mr. Hyde.* Memories that used to retain names, dates, and appointments now hurl them into a murky oblivion, like so many golf balls driven into the dark, squishy folds of a stagnant pond.

In short, this is not a pause that refreshes. Shocking us, as it does, out of midlife complacency with its capacity to distract and debilitate, it could well be called the pause that distresses. Yet thanks to the grace of God and the wisdom of those who have gone before, we can learn to deal with it constructively.

We can become informed. Two books that I've found extremely helpful are *Natural Woman, Natural Menopause,* by Marcus Laux, N.D., and Christine Conrad, and *What Your Doctor May Not Tell You About Menopause,* by John R. Lee, M.D. (recommended by my doctor).* I've also found it valuable (and reassuring) to compare notes with menopausal friends, especially those who have taken the time to educate themselves.

We can take responsibility for our health. Becoming better informed will help us make better choices. We can choose a lifestyle and treatment regimen consistent with our philosophy of health. We can choose health professionals who share, or at least respect, our treatment preferences. With the increased accessibility of natural alternatives, we don't need to feel compelled to limit ourselves to a conventional, one-size-fits-all approach.

We can build on the foundation God has already provided. The eight natural remedies of "pure air, sunlight, abstemiousness, rest, exercise, proper diet, the use of water, [and] trust in divine power" constitute the divinely established foundation for any healthful lifestyle (*The Ministry of Healing,* p. 127). This founda-

tion can be built upon and complemented with appropriate nutritional and herbal supplementation, "bio-
identical," plant-derived prescription hormones, and a
variety of phytohormone-rich foods.

*We can allow God to redeem our distracting, even
debilitating midlife passage into something beautiful.*
Unlikely as it may seem, the timing, the physiological
changes, even the intense moods of menopause, create
an ideal opportunity for prayerful, constructive midlife
assessment. As we feel the ebbing of our youthful vigor,
we're encouraged to rely more on faith, flexibility, and
patience, less on impulse and raw physical energy. As
we confront the record of a life half over, we're invited
to consider soberly how we'll invest the time remaining.
It's a passage we need not navigate alone. If we let Him,
God will work in us to transform our momentary dis-
tress into a promising new beginning.

So there you have it—my take on menopause. If
even one person who reads these words is encouraged
and enlightened, I'll be more than compensated for
publicly baring my menopausal soul. Now if I can just
convince my doubtful, patient husband. (But you knew
I couldn't keep it to myself, didn't you, honey?)

---

* Available in paperback from HarperPerennial and Warner Books, respec-
tively.

Twenty-five

The Wall

*W*arm fuzzies aren't something the rock group Pink Floyd has ever been accused of giving its listeners. Bleak, bitter anthems of alienation and disillusionment wrapped in lush, heavily synthesized arrangements established the band's popularity in the 1970s hugely successful *The Wall,* bassist Roger Waters' dark manifesto of psychological isolation, at once fueled and gave voice to a generation's profound sense of disconnectedness.

So many of us felt like just another brick in a wall—faceless cogs plugged into our designated slots by unseen forces beyond our control. The lyrics matched the circumstances of our lives—random events stacked one upon another, each one compounding and cementing the barriers between us.

Such stark, melancholy messages of alienation tap deeply into the impressionable psyches of unconverted young people. Yet it's startling to realize that similar messages of alienation, crafted in language made palatable for contemporary religious sensibilities, have tapped as deeply into the collective psyche of the church.

On every hand we're regaled with detailed descriptions of our age/gender/race-based differences, instructed as to their significance and severity, and shuttled off to our appropriate subcultures. Pledging allegiance to our patron gods of liberalism, conservatism, health reform, music, political correctness, tolerance,

diversity, [fill in the blank], we war and feud and frag-
ment into a kind of cultural and ideological tribalism.
One wonders where the disintegration will end—perhaps with each member drifting off into a comfortable,
customized congregation of one.

It's not what God had in mind for the body of
Christ. Nearly 2,000 years ago He shattered humanity's
"dividing wall of hostility," making alienation obsolete
(Eph. 2:14, NIV). Through the cross of Christ, He "destroyed the [barriers]" of race, sex, age, temperament,
class, and culture (Eph. 2:14, NIV; see Gal. 3:28). Yet in
order for us to fasten our faith upon that historical reality and make it our own, we need to know more than
what God did—we need to know something about *how*
He accomplished it.

Because alienation is a product of sin, in order to
destroy it Christ first had to uproot the parasitic plant
of sin. And just as every parasitic organism exists
through the life of its host, so it is with sin. It resides in
fallen human flesh, in brain cell and bone marrow, in
the memory banks of our DNA. Just so, it was necessary for Christ to invest Himself in the reality, not just
the resemblance, "of sinful flesh" in order to condemn
"sin in the flesh" (Rom. 8:3).* He condemned and destroyed sin where it resides, by daily denying its inces-
sant urges, by subjecting his opinions and preferences
to the objective scrutiny of the Word, by ultimately surrendering up the sinful self to "the death of the cross"
(Phil. 2:8).

This is what it meant for Christ to overcome alienation in humanity's behalf. If we would share in His vic-
tory, we must confront the sobering reality of what it
means to share in His life of self-abnegation and submis-

sion to the Word and the Spirit of God. Reconciliation and biblical unity come at a price—the price of cherished opinions, of unconverted preferences and practices, of pride and prejudice, of ethnic and cultural loyalties. But what a heaven on earth would unfold before our eyes if we determined to follow the example of Christ!

There would be no more "dividing wall of hostility" between liberal and conservative, contemporary and traditional, young and old, male and female. No more subtle isolationism and alienation. Sharing in a dynamic fusion of that which glorifies God and edifies the body, discarding that which is carnal and self-serving, we would live and worship as Christ intended, in "the unity of the Spirit through the bond of peace" (Eph. 4:3, NIV).

The only question left to be answered is: How badly do we want it?

---

* See *The Desire of Ages:* "When Adam was assailed by the tempter, none of the effects of sin were upon him. . . . It was not thus with Jesus. . . . For four thousand years the race had been decreasing in physical strength, in mental power, and in moral worth; and Christ took upon Him the infirmities of degenerate humanity. Only thus could He rescue man from the lowest depths of his degradation" (p. 117).

Marriage and Family 101

Idealism clings to me as persistently as the scent of a beloved perfume clings to its devoted wearer; we both feel naked without them. Though I was already 28 years old when I quavered "I do," it would have been hard to find a more idealistic young bride who did. A whopping 34 at the birth of our first child, I was the last to know that "naive" was stamped in bold relief across my unsuspecting face. (Our domineering new daughter had no trouble spotting it.)

The idealism remains, but the naïveté has been tempered by repeated run-ins with the gritty realities of day-to-day family life—all of which has yielded an assortment of whimsical and, hopefully, wise observations and suggestions about the basics:

Courtesy is the gentle lubricant of family life. Laughter is its saving grace; affection its lifeblood. Expect great things when they're present.

Pray together daily—many times a day. Identify with and pray for one another's sins, faults, and weaknesses. Practice corporate repentance, and you will become corporately invincible.

Listen.

Cuddling together on the couch and reading *Little House on the Prairie* is 10 times more fun than watching 99 percent of what's on TV.

Be a hotbed of cultural revolution. If "they" say you

can't live on a single income, can't survive without credit cards, and will permanently stunt your children's social development if you deny them quantity time with their peers, don't believe "them." Let the Word and the Holy Spirit be your guides, and make your own way in life.

A small flock of contentedly clucking chickens promotes domestic harmony.

Ingredients of a happy family, according to 5-year-old Jenny: Jesus, Sabbath school and church, lizards and horned toads, sand, when the car runs, worship time, pies without sugar, birthdays, camp meeting, Barbie dolls, Grandma and Grandpa, and having babies (whose, we're not sure; we have no plans).

Tickling is good for the soul.

Unless the house is on fire, a rattlesnake is on the back porch, or the drive shaft fell out of the car at milepost 63, smile when Daddy comes home from work. It means a lot to him.

Husbands, never underestimate a woman's need for personal intimacy, love, and affection. If you do, it may be at the expense of her confidence and respect.

Wives, never underestimate a man's need for physical intimacy, support, and companionship. If you do, it may be at the expense of the affection you so deeply desire.

When you think you've listened long enough, listen some more.

Though it's fallen into some disrepute of late, the old adage "Children should be seen and not heard" has a lot going for it.

A family cat and at least one family dog are vital to a family's mental health. Fish, however, are detrimental; the inevitably dirty tank gives rise to shirking and infighting.

Hormones are not a figment of anyone's imagination; treat each other's with respect.

Elements of a happy family, according to 7-year-old Becky: Jesus, love, cheerfulness (not crabbiness), watching Myrtle (the turtle) eat, Christmas; Bo (the Australian shepherd), Ben (the mutt), Sam (the pampered cat), joy, flowers, the Bible, and a clean house for Mom.

Even if it means doing without, always show hospitality.

If your words are right but your spirit is not, repent quickly and seek forgiveness. If your words *and* your spirit are right, but are misunderstood or unappreciated, give the Holy Spirit time to work—and stand your ground. A false peace is a hollow peace.

Home is the best place in the world for making babies, birthing babies, educating children, feeding and entertaining family and friends, and, I suspect, the best place to die.

When you think you've heard it all and can't bear to hear one more ridiculous, infuriating word, calm down and listen some more.

Never give up on each other. No matter how strained the relationship, how desperate the straits, how hopeless the outlook, we can rejoice that our omnipotent Savior "is able to save *completely* those who come to God through him, because he always lives to intercede for them" (Heb. 7:25, NIV).

Twenty-seven

Turn the Hearts of the Children

No one can ever accuse my mother of not being a good sport. Considering what she's endured over the years to visit us in our various abodes, I marvel at her cheerful determination. Now nearly 70 years old, she still makes the pilgrimage about twice a year. Hauling her stuffed-to-the-gills shocking-pink carry-on through every major Greyhound station in Arizona, casting her lot with penniless college students, greasy mechanics, and gay warlocks* for 10 monotonous hours, she arrives in our backwater—only to place her fragile fate in the bucket seat of our notorious Nissan Stanza.

Only the gamest grandma and mom would subject herself to the vagaries of such a demented car. A car that, to all its other sins, has added this—stranding her on the Interstate en route to the airport, with her flight due to leave within minutes. Thankfully, a police officer materialized and called for a tow truck, then whisked Mom away, leaving me to anxiously ponder her fate. I needn't have worried. She called me that night and gushed, "It was so exciting! The policeman drove me right to the door of the airport—with his siren on! I ran to the gate and stepped on the plane just as the door was closing—I felt just like a movie star!" You have to admire a woman with that kind of chutzpah.

Honestly, though, I haven't always felt that way about it. As an intensely shy child, content to blend with

the furniture of life, I was vexed by my mother's conspic-
uous joie de vivre. And though she never said as much, I
suspect the frustration was mutual. If it weren't for the
blond hair and blue eyes that testified to our genetic
bond, no one would have believed such diametrically op-
posed temperaments could share the same blood.

While I preferred faded jeans and Birkenstocks, Mom
adored hot pinks and gold lamé sandals with jingling
metallic beads. I immersed myself in the company and
conversation of a small circle of close friends; Mom
thrived on parties and dancing and the sweet spice of variety. I dwelled on the serious issues of life and disdained
superficiality; Mom was well acquainted with the seri-
ousness of life and knew the value of a well-timed laugh.

When I became a Christian, I prayed that God would
reconcile our differences. I longed to experience the fulfillment of His end-time promise: "I will send you the
prophet Elijah before that great and dreadful day of the
Lord comes. He will turn the hearts of the fathers [and
mothers] to their children, and the hearts of the chil
dren to their fathers [and mothers]" (Mal. 4:5, 6, NIV).

It's taken some time, but I believe I'm beginning to
hear the faintest whisperings of "the prophet Elijah." I
hear his heartbroken prayer as he fled, exhausted, from
his enemies, "I have had enough, Lord. . . . Take my life;
I am no better than my ancestors" (1 Kings 19:4, NIV).

My heart is learning to take up the refrain: "I have
had enough, Lord—enough of bitterness and alienation;
enough of blame and generational pride. Take my
proud, sinful, self-righteous life, and give me Yours in
its place. I am no better than my ancestors, whose
flaws are mine by inheritance, and whose sins are mine
by choice." Their sins are mine, because no matter

what color or flavor the fruit of sin is, its root of selfishness remains the same. Only a comprehensive repentance that recognizes this universal root can lay the foundation for thorough reconciliation—because it's deep, ingrained selfishness, not uniqueness of temperament and taste, that alienates people and generations.

I pray that someday Mom and I can experience the kind of ultimate reconciliation that comes from a shared vision of the truth. Until then, we can still be the best of friends, cherishing each other's uniqueness. I just wish it hadn't taken me so long to appreciate God's gift to me in this brave, witty, generous, optimistic woman.

Thanks for hanging in there with me, Mom. And next time you come to visit, maybe you could fly, and we'll pick you up in a rental car.

---

* Believe me, I make none of this up.

Twenty-eight

Spiritual Essentials

"You know, honey," I managed to gasp between bone-rattling coughs, "maybe you should just take me out in the desert and shoot me like the broken-down old mare I am."

"Well, now, that's a thought," replied my husband accommodatingly—*a little* too *accommodatingly*, I thought.

I tried a different tack. "Or maybe you could have me quick-frozen and put in cold storage every January, since I always spend it down with the flu anyway. And then you could thaw me out in February when the coast is clear."

"That's another option," Don said, grinning.

My friend Jennifer called from Philadelphia with more pointed threats. "If I were within 100 miles of your place I'd tranquilize you and drag you off to the nearest doctor," she vowed. "It's enough to make a pacifist resort to force."

So much for deferring to the fragile sensitivities of a dying woman!

In any case, when the burning in my asthmatic chest became unbearable and my left lung began to behave like a tightly clamped vise, Jennifer got her wish. I limped into town and presented myself to Cheryl Webb, our kindly nurse practitioner.

Cheryl listened to my lungs, then regarded me in her steady, thoughtful way. "Well, you almost have pneumonia," she said simply. "Let's give you a breathing treatment."

I obediently submitted to the hissing, hookah-like machine and was even glad for the antibiotics I'd tried so hard to avoid. Rugged individualism has a way of biting the dust in the face of certain death.

Yet while the prospect of certain (or at least possible) death galvanizes the sufferer with a certain exhilaration, the tedium of prolonged recovery has a way of sapping the moral fiber. As the dull-as-dust days have dragged into weeks and the near-pneumonia has lapsed into a lingering malaise, I've been forced to do what I've done during so many prolonged illnesses. Take inventory.

When you have just enough energy to brush either your hair or your teeth, but not both, before collapsing back into bed, you have to ask yourself, *What's really essential here?* And as that question generalizes into the broader *What's really essential in life?* all the posturing and calculating you indulged in when you had the energy have a way of fading into the sunset.

The whole ordeal has made me feel, not for the first time in my Christian experience, like a participant in this vision of Ellen White:

"While at Battle Creek in August, 1868, I dreamed of being with a large body of people. A portion of this assembly started out prepared to journey. We had heavily loaded wagons. As we journeyed, the road seemed to ascend. On one side of this road was a deep precipice; on the other was a high, smooth, white wall" (*Life Sketches of Ellen G. White*, p. 190).

As the road grew narrower and steeper, the group was forced to first unhitch the wagons, then cut the remaining baggage from the horses, and finally to abandon the horses. As they proceeded single file on the dwindling path, "small cords were let down from the top of the pure white wall" to help steady them. Finally, barefoot and bloodstained, those who did not turn back found their diminishing path abruptly terminated by a chasm, on the other side of which was "a beautiful field of green grass" suffused by "bright, soft beams of light." They could cross that chasm by one means only—by trusting their entire weight to the cords suspended from God's hand.

As I emerge from yet another lengthy convalescence, I yearn to learn the lesson of the vision more thoroughly than ever before. What to keep and what to cast aside? What proceeds from God and what proceeds from self? I covet the discernment that can distinguish between spiritual essentials and carnal imposters; I pray for the faith and self-discipline to embrace the former while willingly abandoning the latter.

When it's all said and done, we'll go out as naked as we've come in. We'll take nothing that originates from within ourselves. In whatever crucible God refines us, the lesson we must learn is that what does not come from His hand must be left behind. Only He can carry us across the chasm.

Twenty-nine

Prisoner of Love

I'm in love. Wildly, unabashedly, utterly in love. No use trying to be coy and sophisticated about it. My heart has been pilfered by two winsome young imps, and I am a helpless prisoner of love.

I confess that I was smitten from the first. The moment I brought these two into the world and clapped eyes on their perfect, unbelievable frailty, every fiber of my maternal being melted in shameless adoration. From this primal, nurturing love is blossoming an intense appreciation for my daughters' developing individuality and an admiration for the young women of character they're becoming before my eyes.

While babyhood is magical but exhausting and toddlerhood can be charitably described as a brief but terrifying descent into insanity, childhood is a sheer delight. Gone are the midnight feedings and dirty diapers, the impossible energy and indecipherable enunciations. Welcome to the world of delightful discoveries and (semi)rational conversations; of emerging personalities establishing their niche in the family cast of characters.

Seven-year-old Jenny has staked out her role as resident clown and creative genius, daily delighting us with her latest innovations. Unable to find her sheet one morning after kicking it to the bottom of her bed all night, she posted this sign in the hall:

LOST
Sheet. If aneyone finds this sheet
thay will get 2 penneys.

Whimsical and artistic, Jenny can entertain herself
for hours with a bit of string, a scrap of poster board,
and a roll of tape. On a recent hike she discovered a
length of chain, christened it "Ha-Bump," and informed
us that it was her pet snake. When Ha-Bump isn't
slithering around the house sneaking up on unsuspecting prey, "she" can be found lounging in a shoebox,
nestled in a cushy wad of pink tissues.

For Jenny, the thrill is in the chase—in the building, the striving, the learning, the never-ending process
of becoming. The value of the finished product is inci-
dental to the quivering excitement of discovery and creation. An attentive observer of nature and life, she
learns by osmosis, breathing in knowledge and breathing out comprehension as naturally as air.

Big sister Becky couldn't be more different. Literal
and concrete, Becky must have it spelled out, and the
rules that govern "it." For her, the learning process is a
fearful transition from one level of proficiency to the
next—mastery is the thing. Tears of frustration water
her pathway of discovery, but once she gets a thing,
she has it for life.

A gifted organizer and administrator, this energetic
9-year-old has it all under control—balancing home-
work and housework, practicing piano and playing
bossy big sister, caring for our ponies, rabbits, and as-
sorted creatures, and performing a thousand other necessary tasks. Admittedly, ours has never been an easy
relationship, compelled as we both are to try to run the

same household. But despite our significant differences—and our aggravating similarities—we're abso-
lutely and fiercely devoted to each other.

It's been nearly 10 years since I committed myself to
my daughters' care. At times I've questioned the wisdom of my choice. The rigors of making do on a single
income, the frustrations of home-schooling my tempera-
mental carbon copies, the lack of career-related ego
strokes and adult interaction sometimes take their toll.
Sometimes I look wistfully at the lifestyles of peers who
have chosen otherwise, and I confess to more than a little covetousness.[1]

But then I catch the gratitude shining in my daughters' dancing eyes, feel it in their laughing, exuberant
hugs, and even read it in notes shyly slipped into my
hand when I least expect it:

> "Dear Mamma:
>
> "I love you! I think you are the best mamma
> in the whole world! Even though you make me
> do dishes. I hope you keep sleeping every night.[2]
> When I get a big saddle, you can ride Tuffy all
> you want. It will be nice in the new earth when
> you don't have allergies and asthma.
>
> "Love, Becky"

How can I resist the mutual magnetism of such devotion? I don't even try. I am a willing prisoner of love.

---

[1] I understand this works in both directions.
[2] This in reference to a recent bout of midlife-related insomnia.

Welcome to the Human Race

It's been said that every generation needs its confessional singer-songwriter. Perhaps every publisher needs its confessional author. In any case, in this age of unabashed tell-all, I feel compelled to come clean and confess this much: As far as the human race and I are concerned, the honeymoon is over.

It's to be expected, I suppose. Every honeymoon has its heyday, and 40-plus years is a pretty long run. The youthful idealism that carried me through a tumultuous adolescence and catalyzed my early Christian experience has finally evaporated in the heat of repeated disappointment. If I have any faith left in the nobility of human nature, it's a slender scintilla, hanging by a quickly unraveling thread.

How many times can a well-meaning Christian help and share and give, only to be manipulated and unappreciated, without something breaking inside? Who is so emotionally invulnerable as to be unaffected when the promise of friendship turns out to be yet another veiled invitation to an exploitative relationship?

This past year something did break inside. And the pain and disappointment were such that I never wanted to let it happen again. Yet even as I nursed my grudges, I sensed the Lord inviting me to exchange my unrealistic, sentimentalized conceptions of love and friendship for His practical, biblically based principles. So I prayed and studied to discover what Christ understood about love and human nature. This, in part, is what I found.

"But Jesus did not trust himself to them, because he knew all men and needed no one to bear witness of man; for he himself knew what was in man" (John 2:24, 25, RSV). Jesus understood that deep within the heart of fallen humanity "dwelleth no good thing" (Rom. 7:18). Perhaps more important, He also understood that because we are mysteriously ignorant of our supreme selfishness, we harbor untold potential for treachery and exploitation. For this reason, He didn't create unnecessary heartache by burdening people with trusts they were not able to bear.

"By their fruit you shall recognize them" (Matt. 7:16, NIV). Jesus differentiated between Spirit-informed discernment and human judgmentalism. Because of this, He was able to relate to others with eyes wide open to their flaws, strengths, and potential.

"Jesus said to the twelve, 'Do you also wish to go away?'" (John 6:67, RSV). When many disciples became offended at Jesus and left Him, He gave the twelve permission to do the same. Jesus understood that true friendship is based on honesty and freedom, not manipulation or compulsion; that two can walk together only if they're in agreement about what matters most (see Amos 3:3).

"Love your enemies, do good to them, and lend to them without expecting to get anything back" (Luke 6:35, NIV). Jesus didn't set Himself up for continual disappointment by expecting reciprocation from those He loved and served. Though He keenly felt rejection and ingratitude, He was able to persevere in loving the ungrateful and unholy because His own human need for

unlimited, unconditional love was first, and continually, satisfied by the Father.

"Father, forgive them; for they know not what they do" (Luke 23:34). Jesus didn't wait for people to repent, or even to arrive at a complete understanding of how they had offended, before forgiving them. He understood that the consequences of sin and the character flaws that contribute to our predicament can be corrected only in the absence of condemnation and resentment. Jesus understood how to set people free to do better.

"Jesus is not ashamed to call them brothers" (Heb. 2:11, NIV). Choosing "to be made like his brothers in every way," Jesus completely identified Himself with humanity, exempting Himself from no portion of the human experience—except the indulgence of self (verse 17, NIV). He understood that authenticity and humility are vital to experiencing empathy and gaining trust, without which no relationship can thrive.

"Let your light so shine before men, that they may see your good works and give glory to your Father who is in heaven" (Matt. 5:16, RSV). In the final analysis, whether or not we're appreciated, whether or not we're affirmed, we show forth the character of Christ in order to bring glory to God. When we treat others as Christ has treated us, regardless of our reception, we vindicate His character of love in a rebellious world.

The honeymoon was bound to bottom out; as with all honeymoons, it was fed on fantasy, not founded on reality. The thread must be allowed to unravel, because faith placed in the nobility of human nature is a misplaced and ill-conceived faith. Better to entrust our faith to the Savior, who alone

understands how we're made and what we need.
Better to let Him teach us what it means to be a
friend, servant, and member of this intriguing, complex family called the human race.

Thirty-one

Holy Ground

It was one of those average, nondescript days that never make it into the history books. The girls ran out to feed their ponies, only to discover the garden fence stomped to the ground and a half bale of hay mysteriously missing. They didn't need to look far for the culprit. A rogue range cow stood guiltily between the garden and the corral, gazing longingly at what remained of the hay, no doubt planning her next incursion. I chased her off (against the girls' vigorous protests) and parked the car against the gaping hole in the fence. It would have to hold her at bay until Don got home from work.

Meanwhile 8-year-old Jenny decided she was ready to trade me in for another mother. My crime consisted of telling her that as of that night she would no longer be sleeping in her camp cot, but would be moving back to her bunk bed. This was the bunk bed that had been vacated eight months earlier because of an alleged visit from a fruit beetle.

"Honey," I pleaded, "you know the bugs are all gone, and you're a big girl now. You can hardly even get to the closet with this cot in the way, and you'd be much more comfortable in your own bed."

Jenny wasn't buying it. She'd become deeply attached to her cot and wasn't about to give it up without a battle. At breakfast she looked up miserably from her half-eaten oatmeal and said with heartfelt pathos, "I'm not happy with you right now, and I don't want to sit with you."

Sensing that she needed some time to grieve the loss of this piece of her childhood, I let her go in peace.

So it went, this average day, with its average dilemmas—a common thing, unworthy of note by the Master of the universe, who surely had more important things to do than bother with bovine bandits and (allegedly) bug-infested bunk beds. So one would think. And so I was tempted to feel. But somewhere in the middle of it, I read the story of the burning bush, and I saw it again for the first time.

Busy about his duties as a humble shepherd, Moses was attracted by a bush that burned but was not consumed. As he turned aside to view the remarkable sight, the voice of God made this startling announcement, "Take off your sandals, for the place where you are standing is holy ground" (Ex. 3:5, NIV).

Not a common, everyday sight—a mysteriously blazing bush that never burns up. Yet beyond the pyrotechnics that got Moses' attention, God was trying to teach him a deeper truth. It was not from a majestic eminence that God spoke His awe-inspiring words, but from a "lowly shrub, that seemingly had no attractions. This enshrined the Infinite. The all-merciful God shrouded His glory in a most humble type, that Moses could look upon it and live" (*The Desire of Ages,* p. 23).

From a lowly shrub in a desolate desert, in the midst of the common duties of life, God spoke to a common man. Veiling His glory, He drew near, and the ground on which Moses stood became holy.

Through this symbolism God was endeavoring to

teach Moses—and us—something essential about Himself. The Infinite One, Creator of heaven and earth, would find His greatest joy in veiling His glory in the lowly "body of our humiliation" (Phil. 3:21, RV) "that He might draw near to sorrowful, tempted men" *(ibid.).* Casting His lot with frail and faltering humanity, He would identify Himself with our cares and concerns, thereby infusing the common events of our life with grace and holy dignity.

As I saw this lesson of the burning bush through new eyes, my average day didn't seem so average anymore. Not that it looked any different from the outside. Don still had to fix the fence, and Jenny still had to make peace with her bunk bed. The bovine bandit returned with four hefty accomplices to assist her with her next break-in. But the awareness that the infinite God had come near and quietly lived this day with me had transformed the common soil on which I walked into holy ground.

Hospital for Sinners

I have a fear and loathing of hospitals. I know them too intimately. As a severely asthmatic child in smoggy southern California, I visited the emergency room of St. Francis Hospital so regularly the nurses and I greeted each other by name. By the time I married I'd developed such an intense aversion to bright lights and antiseptic smells, I gave birth to my children at home.

So when I recently admitted myself to the local medical center for outpatient surgery, it was with much sighing and trepidation. Though I tried stoically to mask my anxiety, I realized how unsuccessful I was when I glanced up from my bed at the probing face of the anesthesiologist. "Do you have any questions or concerns?" she invited.

"Well, yes," I grimaced, as a nursing student wrestled an IV needle the size of a crochet hook into my vein. "I don't smoke or drink or eat meat, and I weigh only 108 pounds, and I really don't like drugs, so probably the less medication I get, the better."

"I see," she replied gravely, and before I could object she emptied the contents of a hefty syringe into the needle.

"What's that?" I asked with alarm.

"Just a little antianxiety medication," she soothed. As my head began to feel warm and mushy and the contours of the room went wiggly, all the conspiracy theories I had dismissed through the years took on sinister new possibilities. My last semirational thought as I was being wheeled to the operating room was *They haven't put me under yet—I could still run for it!*

But if preparing to be put under was like a bad dream, coming out of the anesthesia was a virtual nightmare. At the sound of my name I reluctantly bobbed to consciousness, only to find myself at the center of an unbearably bright, spinning universe. Sweating and groaning, with eyes and teeth tightly clenched, I fought the overwhelming nausea for what seemed an eternity. Alone, I thought, until a sympathetic voice observed, "You look so miserable."

Surprised, I cracked one eye open just enough to make out the whirling face of a kindly nurse. "Can I have some water?" I croaked.

She obliged by placing a tiny water-soaked sponge on a stick into my parched mouth. Never had a teaspoon of plain water tasted so quenching and luxurious. After that, whenever I rasped for water, the tiny sponge miraculously appeared. And whenever I opened my eyes just enough to discover whether my whirling universe had succumbed to the laws of gravity (it hadn't), I saw that nurse sitting by my side, and I was comforted.

I've often heard it said that the church is not a country club for saints but a hospital for sinners. I've always appreciated that analogy. How true that each of us enters its fellowship morally and emotionally damaged, even diseased, in some fashion. How utterly unentitled we are to despise a fellow "patient" because their deficiencies differ from (or disturbingly mirror) our own.

On the other hand, it also occurred to me as I lay in that reeling recovery room* that if the church is like a hospital, not everyone can be a patient—at least not all of the time. How grateful I was that there were people in that hospital who were well and capable. How comforting it was to see my nurse sitting faithfully by my side, clothed and in her right mind (a phrase that presently didn't describe me), with her sponge-on-a-stick at the ready.

I'm glad the church is becoming a safer haven for wounded souls. It's good to feel the chill of legalistic denial giving way to the warmth of spiritual and emotional honesty. Yet I hope we don't stop short on our road to recovery. Honesty is the first step. Just beyond is a Savior who is able to heal—and a stream of incoming sick and wounded in need of a cool drink of water and the attentive care of recovering wounded healers.

---

* It's true. Even as I writhed in abject misery I found myself mentally composing this chapter. It was then I realized that the brain of a truly hard-core writer is wired such that, if given the chance, we would chronicle—and editorialize—our own funerals.

Thirty-three

Hang On, It Gets Better

"If the only home I hope for is the grave, if I spread out my bed in darkness . . . where then is my hope? Who can see any hope for me? Will it go down to the gates of death? Will we descend together into the dust?" (Job 17:13-16, NIV).

Death and darkness are rapidly settling upon this earth. Courage and optimism, once the express domain of the young, are increasingly replaced by a numbing, enervating hopelessness. For all their unprecedented educational and material advantages, most of these bright, promising young people are tragically ill-equipped to understand why.

All of this was forcibly brought home to my husband and me a few months back. As we chatted over lunch with two young men who'd just moved from St. Joseph, Missouri, we asked the obvious question, "So what brings you all the way to Kingman, Arizona?"

"Warmer weather," shrugged Kevin. "A chance to go someplace new."

Mike had a different answer. "I wanted to get away from all the stuff that's been happening there—like two of my best friends committing suicide within two weeks of each other."

"Suicide—within two weeks of each other?" Don and I asked in shocked unison. "Why?"

"I don't really know. Everything seemed fine. In fact, one of them had everything going for him. Just accepted into the Navy Seals. Always a real straight arrow. But I guess he just felt like he couldn't handle it anymore." Mike shook his head. "He was just 19."

Just 19. A promising, bright young life; a child greatly beloved of God; a soul exhausted by secret torment, seeking permanent relief. As I spooned and swallowed soup that had suddenly turned tasteless, I remembered a day when I was just 18. And I was about to do the same.

I'd come home from school to the usual empty house. Mom was at work; little brother Patrick at the baby-sitter. Dad and my stepmother, Faye, had moved to Arizona; my sisters were off raising families of their own. And in spite of the sunny southern California afternoon, in spite of the comfort and security of my middle-class life, I knew I couldn't handle it anymore.

I couldn't handle the lovelessness and loneliness; the fighting, the alcohol abuse, the multiple bitter divorces, and the strained remarriages. I couldn't handle my overmastering, addictive impulses and the destructive inroads of my death-loving culture.

Wandering to the medicine cabinet, I grabbed a fistful of pain pills and slumped on the fluffy toilet seat. I wondered if there were enough pills to do the job; wondered if I had enough guts to go through with it. And I wondered if anybody would care if I did.

Into these black, satanically inspired thoughts a new voice spoke—a calm, benevolent voice that pleaded with quiet authority. "Hang on," it said simply, "it gets better—I promise."

Sensing that the voice could be trusted, I didn't

argue with it. I simply believed it. "OK," I said aloud. "I'll wait. But it *has* to get better than this—and soon."

It didn't get better soon. The habits and misconceptions of a lifetime didn't fall away overnight; the long, tenacious tendrils of a complex, Christless family legacy were not quickly unraveled. But in time it got just enough better to keep me hoping that it would get better still.

And it keeps getting better. Blessings that a hopeless, alcoholic, drug-abusing misfit once believed were extended only to the favored and the few continue to shower down—blessings of Christian family and friends; of peace and clarity of purpose; of divinely instilled self-respect. Blessings of a glorious, invincible "hope and a future" in Christ (Jer. 29:11, NIV).

Even as death and darkness drape this world as with a burial cloth, all may be assured: "Christ will never abandon those for whom He has died. We may leave Him and be overwhelmed with temptation, but Christ can never turn from one for whom He has paid the ransom of His own life" (*Prophets and Kings*, p. 176).

To any struggling, disheartened brother or sister, young or old, I extend this encouragement: Don't leave His loving embrace. Don't let go of hope. Let His wounded, capable hands minister strength and healing to your trembling ones—and hang on. Though it takes time, it gets better. He promises. And His promises never fail.